Tense and Aspect in Obolo Grammar and Discourse

Summer Institute of Linguistics and
The University of Texas at Arlington
Publications in Linguistics

Publication 128

Publications in Linguistics is a series published jointly by the Summer Institute of Linguistics and the University of Texas at Arlington. The series is a venue for works covering a broad range of topics in linguistics, especially the analytical treatment of minority languages from all parts of the world. While most volumes are authored by members of the Institute, suitable works by others also form part of the series.

Series Editors

Donald A. Burquest
University of Texas
at Arlington

Mildred A. Larson
Summer Institute
of Linguistics

Volume Editors

Marilyn Mayers
Bonnie Brown

Production Staff

Bonnie Brown, Managing Editor
Laurie Nelson, Production Manager
Karoline Fisher, Compositor
Hazel Shorey, Graphic Artist

Tense and Aspect in Obolo Grammar and Discourse

Uche E. Aaron

A Publication of
The Summer Institute of Linguistics
and
The University of Texas at Arlington

© 1999 by the Summer Institute of Linguistics, Inc.
Library of Congress Catalog No: 98-61265
ISBN: 1-55671-063-1
ISSN: 1040-0850

Printed in the United States of America
All Rights Reserved

09 08 07 06 05 04 03 02 01 00 10 9 8 7 6 5 4 3 2 1

No part of this publication may be reproduced, stored in a retrieval system, or transmitted in any form or by any means—electronic, mechanical, photocopy, recording, or otherwise—without the express permission of the Summer Institute of Linguistics, with the exception of brief excerpts in journal articles or reviews.

Copies of this and other publications of the Summer Institute of Linguistics may be obtained from

International Academic Bookstore
Summer Institute of Linguistics
7500 W. Camp Wisdom Rd.
Dallas, TX 75236-5699

Voice: 972-708-7404
Fax: 972-708-7433
Email: academic_books@sil.org
Internet: http://www.sil.org

Contents

Abbreviations ix

Map xii

1 Introduction 1
  1.1 The Obolo people and their language 1
  1.2 The scope of this study 3

2 Overview of Obolo Verbal Morphology 7
  2.1 Obolo as agglutinating language 7
  2.2 Pronominal prefix 10
  2.3 Verb classes 11
  2.4 Mood 12
  2.5 Focus 16
  2.6 Summary 18

3 Tense 19
  3.1 Future tense 19
  3.2 Nonfuture time references 23
  3.3 Futurates 25
  3.4 Genericity 26

4 The Perfect 29
4.1 The perfect in Obolo 30
4.2 The future and past perfect 31
4.3 The polysemy of *rà* 32

5 Aspect 35
5.1 Perfectivity aspect 36
5.1.1 Imperfective aspect 37
5.1.2 Perfective aspect 40
5.1.3 Distribution of the perfectivity aspect 41
5.2 Inherent aspect 42
5.3 Phasal aspect 48
5.4 Co-occurrence of the different types of aspect .. 55
5.4.1 Perfectivity and inherent aspects 55
5.4.2 Perfectivity and phasal aspects 58
5.5 Phasal and inherent aspects 59
5.6 Aspect and tense 63

6 An Overview of Tense and Aspect in Discourse 67
6.1 Domain of tense and aspect 68
6.2 Monologue discourse 69
6.3 Foreground and background in narrative discourse 70
6.4 Grounding in discourse in general 72
6.5 Methodology and terminology 75

7 Tense and Aspect in Narrative Discourse 77
7.1 Tense and aspect in narrative foreground and background . 77
7.2 The data 80
7.3 The structure 80
7.4 Special narrative verb forms 84
7.5 Grounding in the narrative discourse 88
7.6 Tense and aspect in narrative grounding 92
7.7 The concept of a scalar continuum 95
7.8 Summary 98

8 Tense and Aspect in Procedural Discourse 101
8.1 The data 102

8.2 The structure 102
8.3 Grounding in procedural discourse 113
8.4 Tense and aspect in procedural grounding 116

9 Tense and Aspect in Expository Discourse 121
9.1 The data 121
9.2 The structure 122
9.3 Grounding in expository discourse 127
9.4 Tense and aspect in expository grounding 130

10 Tense and Aspect in Expository Compare-and-Contrast
Discourse 133
10.1 The data 133
10.2 The structure 134
10.3 Grounding in compare-and-contrast discourse 136
10.4 Tense and aspect in grounding in compare-and-contrast
discourse. 137

11 Tense and Aspect in Hortatory Discourse 141
11.1 The data 141
11.2 The structure 142
11.3 Grounding in hortatory discourse 150
11.4 Tense and aspect in hortatory grounding 152

12 Summary and Conclusions 155
12.1 Tense and aspect in grammar 155
12.1.1 Tense in grammar 155
12.1.2 Aspect in grammar 156
12.1.3 The perfect 158
12.2 Tense and aspect in discourse 158
12.3 Conclusions 163

Appendix 165
Affirmative verb patterns 165
HTV examples of the verb patterns 172
Negative verb patterns 175
LTV examples of verb patterns 179

References 181

Abbreviations

ACC	Accomplishment	FISH	Fishing text
ACH	Achievement	FISH2	Fishing 2 text
ACT	Activity	FOC	Focus marker
ADV	Advice text	FUT	Future
CANON	Cannon text	G/P	Generic/Perfect Morpheme
CMPL	Completive	GEN	Generic/Genericity
COMP	Complementizer	GENT	Genitive demonstrative
COND	Conditional	H	High tone
CONJ	Conjunction	HAB	Habitual
CONT	Continuous	HL	Falling tone
CONS	Consequential	IFUT	Immediate future
Cpl	Common plural subject prefix	IMM	Immediative
		IMP	Imperative
DANCE	Dance text	IMPF	Imperfective
DEM	Demonstrative	INC	Inceptive
DET	Determiner	INCH	Inchoative
DDEM	Distal demonstrative	INT	Interrogative
DFUT	Definite future	ITER	Iterative
Dstem	reduplication of the verb stem	JUS	Jussive
		L	Low tone
DUR	Durative	NEG	Negative marker
E	time of event	NEUT	Neutral
ES	Elephant text	NSP	Neutralized subject prefix
FIGHT	Fighting text	OR	Oral Rehydration text

OS	Orphan story text	REDUP	Reduplicated syllable
PARA	Paratactic	REL	Relativizer
PDEM	Proximal demonstrative	S	time of speech
PERF	Perfect	SC	School Children text
PFTV	Perfective	SBJ	Subjunctive
pl	plural	SG	Sea God text
POSS	Possessive	sg/s	singular
PREP	Preposition	SP	Subject prefix
PROG	Progressive	STA	Stative
PROGS	Progress text	WARN	Warning text
QUES	Question marker	WB	Wandering Boy text
R	given reference time	WP	White People text

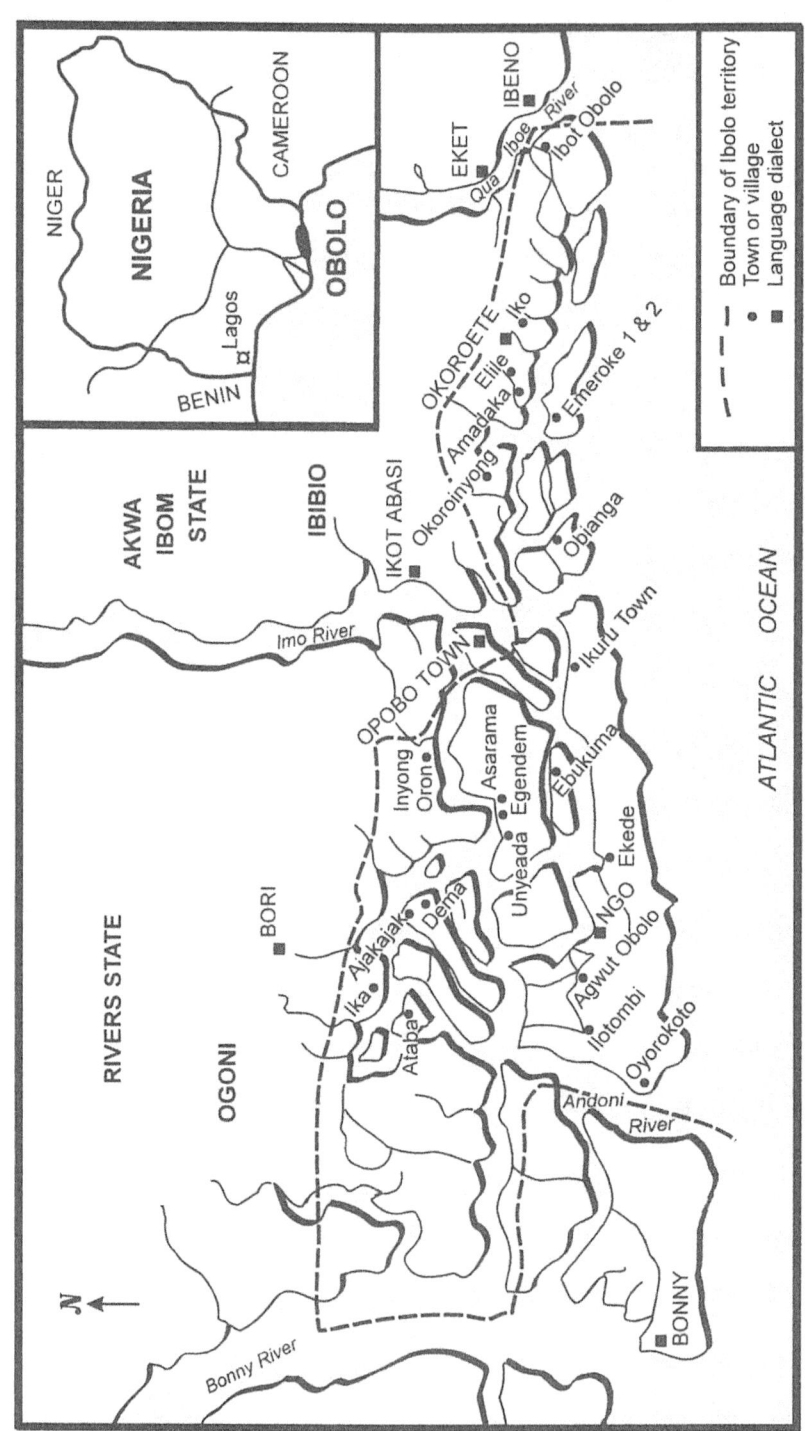

1
Introduction

1.1 The Obolo people and their language

The Obolo (also called Andoni by outsiders), a predominantly fishing people, live mostly on deltaic islands covering and area of about 400 square kilometers on the eastern fringes of the Niger delta on the south eastern coast of Nigeria. The area lies about 4.5° north of the Equator, between the Andoni River and the Qua Iboe River, i.e., between about 7.5° and 8.0° E longitude. Administratively, the people are found in two states, 75 percent in Rivers State and about 25 percent in Akwa Ibom State. Those in Rivers State constitute the Andoni Local Government Area with headquarters at Ngo, while a large part of those in Akwa Ibom State constitute the Eastern Obolo Local Government Area with headquarters at Okoroete. The remaining few villages in the Akwa Ibom State side are administered under the Ibeno Local Government Area. According to projected population figures for 1996 published by the National Population Commission, Obolo people in the two States number about 250,000.

According to Ejituwu (1991), Obolo people migrated from an area called "Irombi" around Bamusso in Ndian Division of the South West Province on the south western coast of the Republic Cameroon, a Bakole (Narrow Bantu) speaking area. Other languages mentioned along the migratory route include Oron, Ibino, Ekit, and Usakade. Linguistic evidence supports this migratory route. However, where they came from before Irombi is questionable linguistically. Some oral traditions claim they came from Egypt to Benin (Afro-Asiatic and Edoid language areas) and on to Irombi. In terms of linguistic classification, Obolo is Niger-Congo, Atlantic-Congo, Volta-Congo, Benue-Congo, Cross River, Delta Cross, Lower Cross West. Bakole, a Narrow Bantu language spoken in the Irombi area, is Benue-Congo, and therefore a distant linguistic relative of Obolo; Oron, Ibino, and Usakade are all Lower Cross languages, and therefore close relatives of Obolo.

Documented records show that long before the British came to Nigeria, Obolo people had contacts with the Portuguese traders as early as 1485 (Ejituwu 1991). The records indicate visits of Portuguese traders in slaves, ivory, etc., in 1699–1704 and in 1867. During the sixteenth century, the Portuguese introduced the Catholic Church in the area; this Christian presence disappeared by the end of the seventeenth century for unknown reasons. It was only in 1870 that the first real converts were made in the western part of Obolo, which led to establishment of the Anglican Church at Ikuru Town around 1900 with a chapel built in 1905. In eastern Obolo (Aaron 1979), the Qua Iboe Mission church was established in Iko in 1911. The Wesleyan Church (now Methodist Church) was established at Amadaka in 1915 and the church established a Primary school at Amadaka in 1918—the first Primary school in Eastern Obolo and one of the first (if not the very first) in the whole of Obolo.

Linguistically, Obolo is bordered on the west by Ibani and Kirike (both Atlantic-Congo, Ijoid languages), on the northwest by Gokana and Khana (both Delta-Cross, Ogoni languages), on the the northeast by Ibibio (Lower Cross East), and on the east by Iko, Ibino, and Ekit (all Lower Cross West languages). On the south is the Atlantic Ocean. Inside Obolo territory there are a few communities that speak Kirike, Igbo (Benue-Congo, Igboid), and Defaka (Atlantic-Congo, Ijoid). The dialects[1] of Obolo include Ataba, Unyeada, Ngo, Okoroete, and Ibot Obolo. Ngo, spoken on the largest island, is the one with the highest rate of mutual intelligibility among all the other dialects. Enene (1998) further subdivided the dialects as follows: Ataba (Ataba), Unyeada (Unyeada, Egendem, Asarama), Ngo (Ngo, Ikuru Town, Ekede, Unyengala-Agana-Egwede, Agwut Obolo, Ilotombi), Okoroete (Okorete-Okorombokho-Okoroiti, Amadaka-Obianga-Emeroke-Amazaaba, Okoroingong-Okoroboile), and Ibot Obolo (Ibot Obolo-Ntafit-Atabrikang 2, Elile, Okorobilom).

---

[1] I refer the reader to Enene (1998) for an exhaustive study of the morphology of Obolo dialects. His work came too late to be properly incorporated into this volume. But it deserves special mention. He refers to Ngo as CENTRAL dialect.

1.2 The scope of this study

The temporal categories of tense and aspect have received much attention in literature. But often scholars concentrate on their grammatical descriptions and functions, without regard to their functions in the discourse. I know of no comprehensive and systematic description of the functions of tense and aspect both at the grammar and discourse levels in any one language. This work seeks to do this for Obolo, a Nigerian language of the Benue Congo family.

In describing tense and aspect in Obolo, my field of inquiry includes both morphological and periphrastic encoding of time references. The periphrastic signals (categories expressed by syntactic means) include temporal adverbials and, especially, serial verbs. For example, the inchoative aspect is marked inflectionally by a prefix *ní* in sequential contexts, and periphrastically by the polysemous serial verb *yákà* 'turn' in nonsequential contexts.

While this study builds on the findings of other linguists who have noticed correlations between certain aspects and the foreground or mainline events of certain discourse types,[2] it stretches them farther, presenting a systematic interaction between tense and aspect in the structure of the foreground and background of all the four main discourse types: narrative, procedural, expository, and hortatory.

The scope of the investigation covers both grammar and discourse levels. The study is done in the framework of functional linguistics. The analysis follows the typology of tense-aspect systems found in the literature to date.[3] At the level of grammar, the study investigates how the language indexes tense, the perfect, and aspect. At the discourse level, the study investigates the function of tense and aspect in the shaping of the structure of the foreground and background of the four main discourse genres.

To carry out these investigations, the following hypotheses were postulated for the grammar and discourse levels. For grammar:

1. That Obolo has a binary tense system with future/nonfuture split, with the future as the marked member and nonfuture unmarked.
2. That there is the category, perfect, in the language, and that it marks current relevance.
3. That three types of aspect are indicated in the language, namely, perfectivity, inherent, and phasal aspects.

---

[2]See Hopper (1979b), Dry (1983), McArthur (1979), Fleischman (1985, 1990), Herring (1991), and Longacre (1983).

[3]See, for example, Reichenbach (1947), Comrie (1976, 1985), Faraclas (1984a), Dahl (1985), Bybee (1985), Bybee and Dahl (1989), Lee (1991), Smith (1991), Binnick (1991), Hopper (1979b, 1982), Dry (1992), Longacre (1989), and Fleishman (1990).

For discourse:

1. That every monologue discourse has foreground (the gist or essential components of the speaker's communicative goal) and background (nonessential material that supports, explains, and facilitates the foreground).[4]
2. That the properties of the foreground of one discourse type are different from those of another discourse type.
3. That tense and aspect play a crucial role in structuring the foreground of each discourse genre and in making it different from that of other discourse genres.
4. That sequentiality, expressed by aspect, is a crucial parameter in distinguishing between discourse types.
5. That the three types of aspect all contribute to the foreground.
6. That the choice of tense and aspect is motivated by discourse, based on the semantic property of the tense or aspect.
7. That the foreground/background distinction is not binary, but scalar in nature, like a continuum.
8. That the foreground is a cluster concept, comprising many categories, not all of which need to be present to qualify a unit, e.g., clause, as a part of the foreground.

The primary database for this study consists of ten texts from the Ngo dialect of Obolo.[5] These comprise four oral and six written monologue texts, representing the four main discourse genres: narrative, procedural, expository, and hortatory. Apart from the general expository, a subtype of this genre, called "compare and contrast" (Fries 1983), was also studied. The oral texts include the Wandering Boy, Fishing2, Cannon, and Advice texts. The written texts include Progress and Warning texts from the *Ida Obolo* (vol. 4, 1992); and the Dance, Fishing, School Children, and Fighting texts from the young people's version of the same magazine called *Ida Obolo Eyi Nsabọn* (vol. 1, 1991). In addition, some examples were taken from other texts, such as White People, Oral Rehydration, both written texts from *Ida Obolo*, (vol. 4, 1992); and oral texts Elephant story, Orphan story, and Sea God story. These oral texts and Wandering Boy were recorded by me in 1984, later published in *Ikpa Urọk* ('Book of Folktales') in 1986.

---

[4]Whether or not interactive discourse types, e.g., conversation, have foreground and background is a subject for another study.

[5]The Ngo dialect is one of five different dialects of Obolo. The others are the Ataba, Unyeada, Okoroete, and Ibot Obolo. Ngo is the one that is most widely understood by speakers of all the other dialects, and the one in which most language development work has been done.

Introduction

In the few places where appropriate data are not found in the database or in any of the secondary texts, elicited data are utilized. There are places where it was necessary to present paradigms. Apart from these examples, the entire study is based on natural texts, both oral and written. Most of the written texts, especially those written by young people, reflect oral styles.

The data were processed using Paradox 3.5, a relational database manager. The texts were divided into clauses, and each clause was coded for several different properties including clause type, tense, and aspect, i.e., phasal, perfectivity, and inherent aspect. I considered the different ways in which temporal structures were indicated in both morphology and periphrasis. Apart from temporal adverbials that mark time reference, most temporal markings are done by means of serial verbs.

Regarding the correlation between forms observed in the data and the meanings they encode, I considered two parameters. First, homogeneity of meaning, where a particular morpheme carries one and the same meaning in all of its occurrences. Secondly, in cases of polysemy, where a form is utilized to encode more than one meaning, I looked for the meaning which is dominant in a given context.

I take the position that speech time or writing time (S) is obligatory, because it is fundamental to all tense, whether absolute or relative. For instance, the very essence of a complex tense rests on the fact that there is more than one reference point. The definition assumed in this study is that tense locates the time of occurrence of a situation (E) sequentially relative to speech time (S), and optionally one or more reference times (R^n). This is given schematically as shown as: Tense = E relative S (relative R^n).

Three levels of aspectual distinctions are observed in the literature, perfectivity aspect, inherent aspect, and the Aktionsarten (Binnick 1991). Linguist are divided as to how many distinctions each recognizes. Some recognize only perfectivity aspect and treat inherent aspect and Aktionsart as inherent meaning. Some recognize both perfectivity and inherent aspects and treat Aktionsart as part of both levels. Very few linguists recognize all three levels.

For a complete taxonomy, it is necessary to include the intermediate group, the Aktionsarten, because its properties are neither all contained in perfectivity aspect nor in inherent aspect. Also, for the purpose of a good analysis, it is good to recognize the group as a separate level.

I recognize three aspectual distinctions, which are referred to as inherent, perfectivity, and phasal aspects. Perfectivity refers to the perfective/imperfective distinction, while inherent aspect refers to the Smith's situation aspect (Smith 1991), and phasal aspect refers to the aspectual meanings (i.e., subphases of a situation) that are classified under the term "Aktionsarten" in the literature. These are fully discussed in chapter 5.

Although it is not possible to separate tense from aspect altogether, for the purpose of presentation I have done just that here.

2
Overview of Obolo Verbal Morphology

This section gives a brief overview of the morphology of the verb[6] in the language, apart from tense and aspect, since these are discussed separately. The discussion here considers the topics of Obolo as an agglutinating language, pronominal prefix, verb classes, mood, and focus.

2.1 Obolo as agglutinating language

By the traditional nineteenth-century morphological typology, i.e., typological classification of languages by structure rather than by genetic affiliation, as revised by Sapir (1921),[7] Obolo may be classified as an

---

[6]An exhaustive treatment of the Obolo verbal morphology is beyond the scope of this study. However, since tense and aspect are indexed morphologically in the language, it is necessary to give a brief overview of the topic. This is the aim of this chapter. For more detailed discussion of some of the points raised here, see *A Grammar of Obolo* by Faraclas (1984a).

[7]For a full description of the history of morphological typology, see Greenberg (1974, chapter 3). As summarized in Croft (1990:40), Sapir (1921) distinguished three types of languages based on the number of morphemes per word: analytic (one morpheme per word); synthetic (a small number of morphemes per word); and polysynthetic (a large number of morphemes, particularly multiple roots, per word). He further distinguished four types of languages based on the degree of alternation of morphemes: isolating (no affixation at all); agglutinative (simple affixation); fusional (considerable morphophonemic alternation); and symbolic (suppletive).

agglutinative (simple affixation) language, with predominantly verbal morphology.[8] According to Bybee (1985:45), in agglutinative languages, morphological boundaries coincide with phonological boundaries, especially syllable boundaries, to an extent that makes segmentation of morphemes transparent. Also, based on the semantic parameter of relevance, Bybee (1985:35) predicts that the order of inflectional morphemes relative to the verb stem is: person—mood—tense—aspect—stem. This order suggests that the aspectual marker is typically closest to the verb stem, followed consecutively by tense, mood, and person markers. These two typological observations are borne out in Obolo. The boundaries of each of the affixes coincide with syllable boundaries, and the general order of morphemes relative to the verb stem agrees with Bybee's order as shown in (1).

(1)   (COND)
            (SBJ)   (NSP)
    (SP)-(G/P)   SP   -(NEG)-(DFUT)-(INCH)-(IMPF)-(STEM)-(REL)-(JUS)
            (INT)   (FUT) (CNS)
            (PROG)

The verbal group, i.e., the verb with all its affixes, as given in (1), is in two parts. The boundary between the two parts occurs between (G/P) and SP, and is indicated by the absence of a hyphen. The first part consists of an optional subject prefix (SP), which is followed optionally by either a conditional (COND) affix, a subjunctive (SBJ) affix, a generic/perfect (G/P) affix, an interrogative (INT) morpheme, or the progressive (PROG) morpheme. The optional SP, when it occurs, obligatorily co-occurs with one of the morphemes following it. It cannot occur in isolation. The second part of the verbal group consists of a string of affixes which begins with another SP or a future (FUT) affix (a portmanteau morpheme which marks both future tense and the subject prefix simultaneously). This second SP becomes a neutralized subject prefix (NSP) if the first part of the verbal group is present. The rest of the structure consists of the negative (NEG) or consequential (CNS) affix, the definite future (DFUT), the inchoative (INCH), imperfective (IMPF), and the verb stem (STEM), which is followed optionally by a relative suffix (REL), and the jussive (JUS) suffix. (The abbreviations here and all others in the book are listed at the front of the book.)

As (1) shows, Obolo is almost exclusively a prefixing language, with only two possible suffixes, i.e., the optional relative suffix, *-bé* (affirmative) and

---

[8]Lehmann (1973), confirmed in Bybee's data (1985), observed that agglutinating languages tend to have SOV as their basic word order. But Obolo, with a basic word order of SVO does not seem to conform with this tendency.

Overview of Obolo Verbal Morphology 9

-bè/-gè (negative), and the jussive morpheme. Obolo combines isolation with agglutination which is observable in the two-part structure of the verbal group, indicated by the absence of a hyphen between G/P and SP. The first part, with its own subject prefix (SP) (except the SBJ marker which does not require a SP) does not contain any verb stem, but rather contains verbal particles, namely the SBJ marker kè, the G/P marker rà, or the PROG morpheme gwú/gwâ (sg) or bí/bâ (pl). In this way its components behave like verbal particles in isolating languages. The presence of an obligatory SP (or NSP) on the next part of the verbal group indicates a new verbal boundary since all verbs in the language begin with a SP (except the imperative which is marked by the absence of a SP). For this reason, the first part of the verbal group is treated as a separate unit and not hyphenated to the second unit. Henceforth, this first part will be referred to as an unbound auxiliary. It is the second part of the verbal group that contains the verb stem. This two-part structure is exemplified in (2) to (5). While (2) and (3) have the two parts, (4) and (5) have only the second part.[9]

(2) î-rà   í-ká   éwé
    3sg-PERF NSP-return market
    S/he has returned (from) market.

(3) kè ǹ-sî   éwé
    SBJ 1sg-go market
    I ought to go to market.

(4) í-sĭ-bô-nĭ-kí-tèm   ínôriè
    3sg-CNS-DFUT-INC-IMPF-cook food
    whenever s/he (begins to) cook food

(5) ǹ-ká-bâ-nù-kí-sí   éwé
    1sg-NEG-DFUT-INC-IMPF-go market
    I shall not (begin) to be going to market.

---

[9]All examples in the work are in the orthography of Obolo (Aaron forthcoming). The sound /ɲ/ is represented as [ny], /ŋ/ as [ñ], and /ɔ/ as [ǫ]. Also, apart from high [á] and low [à] tones, there are also falling [â] and rising [ǎ] contour tones as well as the down-stepped high [!á] and down-stepped fall [!â] in the language. While down-stepped high [!á] is phonologically conditioned, the down-stepped fall [!â] seems to be discourse motivated, as demonstrated in chapters 7 and 8, for the specially reduplicated verbs that occur in sequential contexts. As a result of tone stability in the language, it is possible to have three level tones compressed onto one short vowel. When this happens, it is indicated in the examples as [ȃ], i.e., LHL. See the CV low tone example in (8).

Examples (2) and (3) each show the unbound auxiliaries isolated from the rest of the verbal group by a word boundary. The structural evidence for the word boundary is the fact that the second unit begins with its own SP. The nature of the SP depends on polarity, mood, and the position of the particular verb in the series of verbal elements.

2.2 Pronominal prefix

In Obolo, except for the singular imperative, verbs generally carry bound pronouns, which agree with their subjects in number and person (except for the plural persons where the system is reduced, with only one pronominal prefix for all plural subjects). These bound pronouns are referred to in this study as subject prefixes (SP). The different SPs in Obolo are given in (6). The different forms are alternations due to focus, tense, and mood, as discussed in their respective sections.

(6)   Subject prefixes

	Singular	Plural
1st	N-,[10] ma-	e-,[11] mi-, me-
2nd	o-, mo-	e-, mi-, me-
3rd	i-, o-, mo-	e-, mi-, me-

The SP is obligatory with or without an overt subject noun phrase. In an affirmative indicative serial verb construction, where the subject remains the same, only the first SP alternates to specify person and number. All subsequent SPs neutralize to *í-* as illustrated in (7). They are therefore referred to as neutralized subject prefixes (NSP). The SP *mê-* on the first verb, *sìkì* 'lower' alternates appropriately to agree in number with the plural subject while those on the second and third verbs neutralize to the invariant *í-*.

(7)   èbí   ókwà   mê-sìkì   í-kúp   mé   ágbà
       DET^pl drum   cpl^FUT-lower NSP-stay   PREP   side
       The drummers will sit at the side

---

[10] N is a nasal homorganic with the immediately following consonant.

[11] In the Ngo dialect, most speakers replace the common plural *e-* with *i-* in relative and conditional clauses. Also, in the imperative the 2pl subject is indicated by the low tone *ì-* in all dialects. Since *ì-* is not used to refer to 2pl in any other context, it is hard to say whether it is, indeed, indicating 2pl or just plurality, as in the Ngo dialect.

í-kí-kwák   ókwà
NSP-IMPF-beat drum
beating the drums.

Basically SPs neutralize anaphorically to indicate sameness of subject, that is, where the subject is recoverable from the preceding discourse. When a new subject is introduced, the system starts all over again with an appropriate inflection on the first verb followed by the neutralized form on subsequent verbs as shown in (8).

(8) gwúñ yà   ó-sâ-sà   èsé   yà   í-jé
     child DDEM^s 3S^FOC-REDUP-take crayfish DDEM^s NSP-walk
     The boy walked away with the crayfish

     í-sí   í-ré   érè   ògbògbò ǹsàbón   íríèèñ é-sìkí-bé
     NSP-go NSP-reach place many   children male   CP^FOC-lower-REL
     up to the place where many boys sat down

     í-kwéék í-kí-tó   úkọ́ọ́k
     NSP-sit NSP-IMPF-cast hook
     (and) were casting (their) lines.

In (8), the SP on the first verb inflects to agree in number (singular) and person (third) with the first subject, gwúñ yà 'the boy', and subsequent SPs that are coreferential with it, all neutralize to indicate same subject until a new subject is introduced. When the new subject, ògbògbò ǹsàbón íríèèñ 'many boys' is introduced, the SP on the first verb after it, é-sìkì-bé 'sit down' inflects appropriately to agree in number (plural) with it, and the SPs on the next verbs, í-kwéék 'sit' and í-kító 'cast' neutralize to indicate sameness of subject with the first verb. These facts suggest that Obolo is a type of switch reference language, that is, a language in which each clause is marked to indicate whether it has the same or different subject from a reference clause. In Obolo the reference clause seems to be the previous clause, whether within the same sentence or in the sentence before the one in question. While prototypical switch reference languages mark both same subject and different subject morphosyntactically, Obolo marks only same subject.

2.3 Verb classes

Generally, Obolo verbs divide into two classes based on their stem tones. That is, every verb belongs either in the high or low tone class. Most verbs are either monosyllabic, of the forms CV, CVC, or CV:C, or disyllabic CVCV. All trisyllabic verbs are derived forms which encode iterative plurality (Aaron 1996/97). The tones on each verb stem alternate in accordance with the tone class and syllable pattern of the verb to indicate mood, focus, and polarity. The imperative form of the two verb classes, as well as the different syllable patterns are illustrated in (9), showing the characteristic imperative HL pattern for high tone class and LHL pattern (LH for CVC) for low tone verbs (see §2.4). The tone pattern distributes itself over multiple syllable verbs and contract over monosyllabic verbs, resulting in three tones on a single syllable low tone verb as illustrated in (9).

(9)
Syllable pattern	High tone class	Low tone class
CV	rê ámà reach town arrive at (the) town	rè̂ àtá énê be good person be a good person
CVC	típ ìkpòkò contribute money contribute money	tĭp úfè set trap set a trap
CV:C	tíík énê abuse person abuse a person	tǐìk énê eulogize person eulogize a person
CVCV	kpókò̩ íyé split firewood split the firewood	kpòkò̩ énê knock person knock a person (with a fist)
Verb focus[12] CVCVCV	kpókpókò̩ íyé **split** firewood **split** the firewood	kpòkpókò̩ énê **knock** person **knock** a person (with a fist)

2.4 Mood

In Obolo, modality is marked morphologically by verbal inflections, syntactically by serial verb constructions, and semantically by lexical

---

[12]When the verb receives focus in the language (see §2.5), the verb stem is reduplicated resulting in a CVCVCV pattern for two syllable verbs.

items. Only modality categories that are morphologically marked on the verb are discussed here. These include the indicative, imperative, hortative, subjunctive, consequential, conditional, interrogative, and jussive.

The indicative mood. The indicative in Obolo is the unmarked mood. There is no special morpheme, segmental or tonal, on the verb which marks the indicative mood. In exemplifying moods, I have decided to illustrate the high and low tone verb class paradigm using a high tone CVCV verb, *chílí* 'open', and a low tone CVCV verb, *chìbî* 'scoop', to show the similarities and differences in the marking of each type. An example of indicative sentence is given in (10).

(10)   ń-chílí   òtíñ   ń-chìbí   ùsùñ
       1sg-open pot   1sg-scoop soup
       I opened the pot.   I scooped some soup.

The imperative mood. The imperative is marked by the absence of a subject prefix in the singular and a low tone subject prefix ì- in the plural. Imperative verb stems carry a specific tone pattern.[13] Final high (H) tones over two-syllable verbs become low (L) for high tone verbs and falling (HL) for low tone verbs when the object is zero, and remain high when an overt object is present, as in (11a) and (11b). In the plural, both high and low tone CVCV verbs carry a HL pattern, with or without an object, as in (11c).

(11)   a. *chílì*   *chìbî*
          open   scoop
          Open (it)!   Scoop (it)!

       b. *chílí òtíñ*   *chìbí ùsùñ*
          open   pot   scoop   soup
          Open the pot!   Scoop some soup!

       c. *ì-chílì   òtíñ*   *ì-chìbì   ùsùñ*
          2pl-open pot   2pl-scoop soup
          Open the pot (you pl)!   Scoop some soup (you pl)!

Imperatives may be marked for contrastive verb focus as shown in (12a) and (12b), by reduplicating the verb stem. The reduplicated syllable carries the stem tone while the rest of the stem carries the imperative HL tone pattern.

---

[13]The phonological derivation of this and other grammatical tone patterns is beyond the scope of this work. Only relevant descriptions will be given here.

(12) a. chí-chílì   òtíñ   chì-chíbì   ùsùñ
        REDUP-open pot   REDUP-scoop soup
        Open the pot!   **Scoop** some soup.

    b. ì-chí-chílì   òtíñ   ì-chì-chíbì   ùsùñ
       2pl-REDUP-open pot   2pl-REDUP-scoop soup
       Open the pot (you pl)!   **Scoop** the soup (you pl)!

The hortative mood. The hortative verb stems carry the same tone pattern as the plural imperative. The only morphological difference between them is the form and tone pattern of the SP. For hortative, the SP is ñ̀- for 1sg, ò- for 2sg, í- for 3sg, and é- for all plural.

(13) í-chílì   òtíñ   í-chíbì   ùsùñ
     3sg-open pot   3sg-scoop soup
     Let him/her open the pot.   Let him/her scoop some soup.

The subjunctive mood. The subjunctive mood is marked by the morpheme *kè* and a HL and LL tone pattern on high and low verb stems, respectively. The subjunctive morpheme *kè* precedes the SP and a full subject NP may come in between them. The SPs *n-, o-,* and *e-* carry a low tone before high tone verbs and high tone before low tone verb stems.

(14) kè énê ò-chílì   òtíñ   kè énê ó-chìbì   ùsùñ
     SBJ Ene 3sg-open pot   SBJ Ene 3sg-scoop soup
     Ene should open the pot.   Ene should scoop some soup.

The consequential mood. The consequential mood is marked by the morpheme *-sĭ-* with a rising tone. The verb stem retains its basic tone pattern, i.e., HH for high tone verbs and HL for low tone verbs. The consequential in Obolo is classified as a subordinating mood because it occurs only in subordinating clauses.

(15) í-sĭ-chílí   òtíñ   ì-sĭ-chìbí   ùsùñ
     3sg-CONS-open pot   3sg-CONS-scoop soup
     whenever s/he opens the pot   whenever s/he scoops some soup

The conditional mood. The conditional is also a subordinating mood. It is closely related to the consequential mood in that, except for the consequential function, the consequential could generally be classified as the WHEN condition while the conditional could be classified as the IF condition. In the former, the speaker is certain that the condition will come to pass, but in the latter he is not sure. Both are also irrealis.

Of all the moods, the conditional is the only one that is sensitive to tense changes: future and nonfuture. The conditional morphemes alternate for tense. Future conditional mood is marked by the optional conditional word *íré* 'if' in the subordinate protasis (i.e., the hypothetical clause) and the future tense inflection on the main verb in the apodosis (i.e., the consequence clause) in the conditional sentence. This is illustrated in (16).

(16)   *íré í-riá*   *èmì mâ-sì*
        if   3sg-send   1sg   1sg^FUT-go
        If s/he sends me, I will go.

Past conditional mood listed in (17) is marked by a high-tone portmanteau morpheme *mV-* which marks both the SP and past conditional as exemplified in (18).

(17)   Paradigm of past conditional morpheme

        má-   1sg
        mó-   2/3sg
        mé-   all pl

(18)   *mó-riá*   *èmì má-sí*
        3sg^COND-send   1sg   1sg^COND-go
        If s/he sent (had sent) me, I would go.

The interrogative mood. The only type of interrogative mood that is marked on the verb is the HOW question. It is marked by reduplication of the verb stem, with a low tone on all singular SP *ǹ-, ò-, ì-*, and a high tone on the common plural SP *é-*. The tone pattern on the stem is HL fall on the reduplicated syllable followed by LL on the stem for both high and low tone verbs.[14]

(19)   *ì-chî-chìlì*   *òtíñ*   *ì-chî-chìbì*   *ùsùñ*
        3sg-REDUP-open pot   3sg-REDUP-scoop soup
        How did s/he open the pot?   How did s/he scoop some soup?

---

[14]The tone on the high tone verbs becomes low because phonologically the falling tone lowers all succeeding high tones in the phrase, i.e., it changes all succeeding high tones to low tones. It has no effect on succeeding low tones because they are already low.

The polar question is indicated by means of the optional low tone question word ìrè (lit: 'it be') placed in the unbound auxiliary slot, as exemplified in (20).

(20) ìrè î-chìlì òtíñ   ìrè î-chìbí ùsùñ
      QUES 3sg-open pot   QUES 3sg-scoop soup
      Did s/he open the pot?   Did s/he scoop some soup?

The jussive mood. The jussive is a grammatically defined class of sentences characteristically used to (politely) issue commands, demands, requests, entreaties, etc. The jussive suffixes, *mà* for commands, *ní* for questions, and *ou/ei* for entreaty, are suffixed to the verb root when there is no overt post-verbal NP, as illustrated in (21a). When there is a post-verbal NP, the jussive is suffixed to it, rather than to the verb, as illustrated in (21b).

(21) a. *chílí-mà*   *chìbí-mà*
         (2sg)^IMP-open-JUS   (2sg)^IMP-scoop-JUS
         Open please/then.   Scoop please/then.

      b. *ì-chî-chìlì*   *òtíñ-ní*   *ì-chî-chìbì*   *ùsùñ-ní*
         3sg-REDUP-open pot-JUS   3sg-REDUP-scoop soup-JUS
         How did s/he open the pot   How did s/he scoop the soup
         please/then?   please/then?

2.5 Focus

Faraclas (1984a:59, 1984b) defines focus in Obolo as referring to that part of the sentence which receives the emphasis of the speaker. However, because of the unrevealing nature of the term emphasis, this definition needs to be modified as that constituent of the sentence which the speaker marks as, or considers to be, most pragmatically salient in the communication situation.

Languages mark focus by stress and intonation, morphology, word order, and certain syntactic constructions. In Obolo, I am concerned with focus as it is marked in the morphology of the verb. Faraclas (1984:59-60) has distinguished two focus systems on Obolo verbs. The first contains prefocus (i.e., when the speaker focuses on elements occurring before the verb, e.g., subject) and postfocus (i.e., when the speaker focuses on postverbal elements such as direct object and obliques like temporal or locative NPs). The second contains verb focus (i.e., when the speaker focuses on the action or state expressed by the verb) and auxiliary focus (i.e., when speaker focuses

Overview of Obolo Verbal Morphology   17

on auxiliary elements such as aspect). He also points out that any verb may be neutral with respect to any or both of these focus systems. Some very basic examples of the focus systems are given in (22) to (26). Except for (22), all the examples carry contrastive focus. A constituent under contrastive focus also falls under assertive focus, but not vice versa. Therefore, (23) to (26) also carry assertive focus.

Neutral focus. Although Faraclas classifies this as a neutral focus form, it actually corresponds to assertive focus in the literature.[15] It is also the form that is used to express counter-assertive polar focus, i.e., the truth value 'true', which the speaker asserts to contradict hearer's utterance that the truth value is 'false' for the sentence. For the latter meaning, the SP receives an artificial stress to indicate this pragmatic function. This focus form is marked by different forms of the SP (ń- for 1sg, ó- for 2sg) with the verb retaining its basic tone pattern, except for 3sg (î-) and common plural form (mî) whose falling tone induces a phonologically conditioned low tone on the following high tone syllable. This form is illustrated in (22) where the basic tone of the verb 'to go' is high.

(22)   ǹté î-sì   éwé   ń-sí   éwé
       Nte 3sg-go market   1sg-go market
       Nte went to market.   I went to market.

Postfocus. When the focus is on a postverbal element, e.g., locative NP, the form of the 3rd sg SP changes to ì-, i.e., i- with a low tone, and the verb stem retains its basic tone pattern, here high tone. In (23) the focus is on the postverbal locative NP, éwé 'market'. Subject prefixes other than 3sg become ǹ-, ò-, and é- for 1sg, 2sg, and common plural forms, respectively.

(23)   ǹté ì-sí   éwé   é-sí   éwé
       Nte 3sg-go market   cpl-go market
       Nte went to **market**.   We/you/they went to **market**.

Prefocus. When the speaker focuses on the subject, a preverbal element, the third person singular SP becomes a high toned ó- and the stem tone remains in its basic form, here high. In this focus form, unlike any other, the subject must be obligatorily stated, whether as a noun or independent pronoun, along with the SP. Other SPs are ń-, ó-, and é- for 1sg, 2sg, and common plural forms, respectively.

(24)   ǹté ó-sí   éwé   òwù ó-sí   éwé
       Nte 3sg-go market   2sg 2sg-go market
       Nte went to market.   **You** went to market.

---
[15]See Watters (1979:49) and Givón (1990:699).

Auxiliary focus. When an auxiliary element such as aspect is in focus, its marker is reduplicated. The SPs for this focus form are ǹ-, ò-, ì-, and é- for 1sg, 2sg, 3sg, and common plural forms, respectively. In (25a) where the focus is on the imperfective aspect, the marker kí- is reduplicated. Modal elements may also receive focus as illustrated for the subjunctive mood in (25b). Here the subjunctive morpheme kè is reduplicated.[16]

(25) a. ǹté ì-**ké-kí**-sí   éwé   ǹ-**ké-kí**-sí   éwé
        Nte 3sg-REDUP-IMPF-go market   1sg-REDUP-IMPF-go market
        Nte **does** go to market.   I **do** go to market.

   b. **ké-kè**   ǹté ò-sî   éwé   **ké-kè**   ǹ-sî   éwé
      REDUP-SUBJ Nte 3sg-go market   REDUP-SUBJ 1sg-go market
      Nte **should** go to market.   I **should** go to market.

Verb focus. As with the auxiliary focus, the focused morpheme, here the verb stem, is reduplicated. But the verb stem tone becomes HL,[17] while the reduplicated syllable retains the basic tone of the verb, here high tone.

(26) ǹte ì-**sí-sî**   éwé   ǹ-**sí-sì**   éwé
     Nte 3sg-REDUP-go market   1sg-REDUP-go market
     Nte **went** to (not returned from) I **went** (not returned from)
     market.   market.

2.6 Summary

Obolo is an agglutinative, mainly prefixing language. Every verb, except singular imperative verbs, carries a bound pronominal subject prefix which agrees in number and person (except plural form) with the subject. The verbs fall into two classes depending on their stem tones—high or low—and they inflect for polarity and mood in accordance with their stem tones and syllable patterns. Apart from tense, aspect, and mood, the phonological shape and tone of the verb may also be affected by focus.

---

[16]As usual with verbs with the high vowel *i*, the vowel of the reduplicated syllable is lowered to *e*.

[17]On a two-syllable verb stem, this HL tone pattern spreads itself over the two syllables.

3
Tense

My analysis indicates that Obolo has a binary tense-marking system with a two-way, future/nonfuture, split. It consistently expresses the future time with a particular morphological marking that belongs only in the temporal (future tense) paradigm. It is not an irrealis/realis split for the following reasons. First, the future tense morpheme, for instance the falling tone *mV*, is only used to indicate futurity. It is not used to indicate presumption or prediction in any other time reference. Secondly, nonfuture irrealis does exist in the language, e.g., tense-neutral subjunctives, and conditionals, but these do not carry any of the morphemes that mark the future, namely, *mV, bV, kpV,* all with falling tones. Thirdly, any of these irrealis elements may be used without prediction, but the future tense markers are never used without prediction. The future tense only indicates irrealis because the events expressed in the future are not yet realized. Therefore, there may be instances where the irrealis meaning of the future marking is in focus. But this is not the primary meaning of these morphemes. The two-way split system is discussed below, first the future, then the nonfuture.

3.1 Future tense

The definition of future tense adopted in this paper, is illustrated in (27), where E stands for time of the event, R for a given reference time, and S for time of speech.

(27) Future tense: E(,R) after S

or --|-----+--->
    S   E(,R)

However, this definition fits more than one morpheme in the language. One of these, *mV-* with a falling tone, marks simple future while the other morphemes and combination of morphemes mark modally qualified future tenses. These are discussed below.

Simple future. The simple future tense is marked by a portmanteau morpheme, *mV-* with a falling tone, which encodes both the SP and the future tense. The vowels alternate in the paradigm for person and number as shown in (28). In my database, all occurrences of the falling tone *mV-* serve the single purpose of encoding the simple future, an example of which is given in (29).

(28) Paradigm of future marker

    mâ- 1sg
    mô- 2/3sg
    mê- all pl

(29) **mâ-sì**   ákộñ
    1sg^FUT-go battle
    I will go to battle.

Simple negative future. Negated simple future is marked with a different portmanteau morpheme, *kpV-* with a falling tone, as given in (30), with an example of negative simple future given in (31). This morpheme, in all its occurrences, does not mark anything else other than the negative future.

(30) Paradigm of negaative future marker

    kpâ- 1sg
    kpô- 2/3 sg
    kpê- all pl

(31) lêì!   ò-**kpô-kột**   í-rọ́
    wow 2sg-FUT^NEG-able NSP-do
    Wow! You will not be able to do it.

Definite future. Definite future indicates that the event will definitely come to pass, and/or that it will come to pass at a definite time. The morpheme *bV-* with a falling tone, from the verb *bé* 'say', has grammaticized to a future marker. It layers[18] with the falling tone *mV-* (future marker) and has the meaning of definite future marker; the speaker is offering an assurance that an event will take place at some definite time. As with *mV-* and *kpV-*, the vowels of *bV-* alternate for person and number as shown in (32).

(32) Paradigm of definite future marker

bâ- 1sg
bô- 2/3sg
bê- all pl

The morpheme, *bV-* with a falling tone, however, does not always mark definite future. Being a gram[19] that has not yet completely grammaticized, *bV-* may also mark intention. Distinguishing between definite future and intention is one of the instances where the notion of contextually dominant meaning is applied. There will, of course, be instances where the meaning is indeterminate between definite future and intention.

In example (33), future time reference is the dominant parameter in 'being able to join the dance group' and the intention meaning does not seem to be at issue. By applying the Gricean principle of conventionalization of implicatures to example (34), however, the issue there is the "revealing of intention" although the notion of the futurity of the time when the intention will be realized is not excluded from the meaning. So, (33) is an example of definite future while (34) is an example of intention with future tense reference as a secondary meaning focus.

(33) òwù ò-ká-**bô**-kọ̀t í-gọ̀ọ́k í-fìt
2sg 2sg-NEG-DFUT-able NSP-follow NSP-play
You are not going to be able to join the dance group.

(34) ògwú òbòlò ì-kí-kpá ínû gèèlék
DETˆsg Obolo 3sg-IMPF-tell thing every
The Obolo person used to tell everything

---

[18]Layering is a term which expresses a situation where a newly grammaticized morpheme coexists with an old one to express the same meaning.

[19]The term 'gram' is used by Bybee, Pagliuca, and Perkins (1994) as a short form for "grammatical morphemes" or morphemes which are formed from lexical items through the process of grammaticization.

ì-**bô**-rọ̀   í-nyí   ògwú   ókólóbô
3sg-INT-do NSP-give DET^sg Okoloba
he intended to do to the Okoloba person.

Immediate future. Apart from occurring by itself as a single morpheme, *mV* may also be combined with the inchoative morpheme, *ni*,[20] to encode the immediate future. The combination of *mV* and *ni* translates best into the English 'to be about to'. The description of the function of this future type and the morphemes that mark it in Obolo fits well the classification of immediate future as described by Bybee, Pagliuca, and Perkins (1991:415–419). They include the verb "come" as one of the primary sources from which grams that mark it are derived. The immediate future paradigm is given in (35). An example of the immediate future is given in (36).

(35)   Paradigm of immediate future morpheme

    mâ-nĭ-   (fast speech *má!ní-*)   1sg
    mô-nĭ-   (fast speech *mó!ní-*)   2/3sg
    mê-nĭ-   (fast speech *mé!ní-*)   all pl

(36)   ké   ọ̀mộ   **mô-nĭ-tàp**   gwúñ   kàñ   mé   úwù-íkpá
    COMPL 3sg 3sg^FUT-put child 3sg^POSS PREP school
    that he was about to put his child in school

When this combined morpheme co-occurs with the temporal adverbial *săbùm* 'before', however, it ceases to mark the immediate future. The reason is that *săbùm* 'before', which would fall into the same category as the English verbs *start, go on*, etc., delays the imminence of the future event and focuses on the phase before the situation. An example of *săbùm* interfering with the function of *mônĭ* is given in (37). In this example, although owning the boat is still a future situation, it has lost its imminence.

(37)   **săbùm**   òwù   **mó-!ní**-kááñ   újí
    before 2sg 2sg^FUT-INCH-have canoe
    Before you have a boat

---

[20]See §5.5 for *ni* as an inchoactive aspect marker. The morpheme *ni* has probably grammaticized from the indicative form of the verb *nu* 'come' (imperative *nă*). In the indicative immediate future construction, *nu* obligatorily precedes the verb in a clause chain, and the verb obligatorily carries the NSP *í-* (as in mâ-nù í-tàp 'I am about to put'). In fast speech, vowel elision occurs across the word boundaâry, *deleting ù* in favor of *í* and leaving behind its low tone which in turn combines with the high on *í* to create a rise on the *i*, resulting in *nĭ* as in [mâ-nĭ-tàp] with the characteristic rising tone as shown in (35).

3.2 Nonfuture time references

The fact that Obolo has a binary future/nonfuture split, and only has morphological marking for the future tense, is confirmed by the use of temporal adverbials in the language. Two texts in my database, PROGS and WB, were studied for this feature and the results are given in (38). It is not necessary to describe futurity by means of temporal adverbials because it is already marked morphologically on the verb. Past and present time references, however, are not so marked and thus use temporal adverbials to mark them (though not often) and to distinguish them from each other.

(38) Use of temporal adverbials

Text	Total	Past	Present	Other
PROGS	22	7	10	5
WB	8	2	0	6

The PROGS text, being a compare and contrast text, involves a variety of tenses—future, past, and present. Of the five future time references in the text, none was marked by means of temporal adverbials, but rather all were marked morphologically on the verbs. The past and present time references were all marked by means of temporal adverbials. On the other hand, the WB text is a past tense narrative in which the past temporal orientation is given at the beginning of the story and sets the time reference for the entire story.

In general, however, some present and/or ongoing situations may be referred to without temporal adverbials. Faraclas (1984a:62) posits a present tense marked by the morphemes *gâ* (sg) and *bâ* (pl) in Obolo. These morphemes occur as optional parts of the marking of the progressive aspect (see §5.1), and they also occur with past temporal adverbials. Therefore, they do not mark present tense. Except for the periphrastic marking with temporal adverials, Obolo does not mark the present tense. Situations reported at time of speech are either states (perfectives without endpoints or perfect with currently relevant states) or ongoing situations at the time of speech.

Two types of situations may be said to be in the PRESENT in Obolo: a present state and an ongoing situation. The present state is expressed by a nonfuture perfective stative verb, as illustrated in (39), while the ongoing situation may be habitual or progressive, as illustrated in (40) and (41).

(39) òbòlò î-jàáñ
Obolo 3sg-beautiful
Obolo is beautiful.

(40) èjì mî-kì-sì m̀bọ́m
1pl cpl-IMPF-go fishing
We (habitually) go fishing.

(41) mé àtíkộ òbòlò ò-kí-bóló
PREP truth Obolo 3sg-IMPF-wake^up
Truly, Obolo is waking up.

However, these are all default cases of time indication. Without temporal adverbials, they indeed express present time indication. But the same morphological forms will carry a different time reference with a nonpresent temporal adverbial or phrase, as illustrated in (42) to (44) with a past temporal phrase.

(42) m̀gbọ̀ ò-râ-ràkà òbòlò î-jàáñ
time 3sg-REDUP-pass Obolo 3sg-beautiful
In the past, Obolo was beautiful.

(43) m̀gbọ̀ ò-râ-ràkà èjì mî-kì-sì m̀bọ́m
time 3sg-REDUP-pass 1pl cpl-IMPF-go fishing
In the past, we (habitually) went fishing.

(44) m̀gbọ̀ ò-râ-ràkà òbòlò ò-kí-bóló
time 3sg-REDUP-pass Obolo 3sg-IMPF-wake^up
In the past, Obolo was waking up.

Due to this fact, it becomes necessary at times, to include present temporal adverbials to ensure the present time meaning, as illustrated in (45).

(45) mé égwê chérékèyí èjì mî-kì-sà m̀kpá èbí ǹgwâñ
PREP day today 1pl cpl-IMPF-take death DET^pl sibling
Today...we do use the death(s) of our siblings

    kìjì í-tàp òchìchâ í-nyí lék kìjì
    1pl^POSS NSP-put enmity NSP-give body 1pl^POSS
    to create enmity for ourselves.

The present adverbial may also be used to indicate currently relevant states that result from previous situations, as illustrated in (46).

(46) mə́jè   ówùwà   únwèné î-nùñ̄   mé èmèn òbòlò mé
     because many   change 3sg-enter PREP inside Obolo PREP

   chérékèyí
   today
   because many changes have entered Obolo today

From these examples, it is clear that the present tense is not morphologically marked in Obolo. The verb forms that carry present meaning only do so by default. With nonpresent temporal adverbials or phrases, the same morphological forms will carry nonpresent meanings.

3.3 Futurates

In Obolo, there are also mixed time references such as "past in the future" and "future in the past" (Comrie 1985), which are among the group of complex tenses that are collectively referred to as futurates in literature. They are indicated by a combination of appropriate temporal phrases or adverbials which form the reference time, R, and an appropriately marked verb. Temporal adverbials play a crucial role in the coding of temporal notions in languages that do not have morphological inflections for tense.

The past in the future in Obolo is indicated by a combination of future temporal reference and the nonfuture perfective form. The future temporal reference may be either a future temporal adverbial or a relative time fixed by a specified future situation. This is exemplified in (47).

(47) (săbùm) ìké m̀gbò̩ kèyí ìyâkwùt î-kă̆   éwé
     (before) limit time PDEM tomorrow 3sg-return market
     (Before) this time tomorrow, s/he has (i.e., will have) returned from market.

The future in the past is illustrated in (48). In the absence of any specific past tense inflectional morphology, it is indicated by a combination of past temporal phrase in the first part of (48) and a future tense inflection on the verb in the second part.

(48) m̀gbò̩ î-nù-bè   m̀-bâ-sì   éwé
     time 3sg-come-REL   1sg-DFUT-go market
     When s/he came, I was going to go to market.

Without any predefined temporal frame and without any temporal adverbial or phrase, such an expression is also interpretable as future in the future. Example (49) is from a narrative in the past. But, outside of its past narrative context, it has both a past and a future meaning: 'before he came out' or 'before he will come out.'

(49) sằbùm mó-!ní-sìbí   í-nú
     before 3sg^FUT-INCH-come^out NSP-come
     before he came (or will come) out

3.4 Genericity

Before leaving the topic of tense, it is worth mentioning that Obolo has a system of expressing an event as generic. This can be done by means of the polysemous morpheme *rà* within and out of any predefined time reference as illustrated in examples (50) to (52). The morpheme *rà*, apart from expressing genericity, also encodes the perfect (see also chapter 4). A verb marked with *rà* assumes the dominant tense in the context in which it occurs. If *rà* occurs in the context of a narrative, or in the vicinity of any time phrase, the verb it co-occurs with has the time reference expressed by the narrative context or the time phrase as illustrated in (50) and (51). Example (50) is taken from a folktale, where an orphan makes a living by going from town to town with a finger of his dead father in a small bag, asking people to mention what is in the bag or pay him a stipulated sum of money. The narrative tense is the distant past which is already indicated at the beginning of the story. In this story, -*rà* in (50b) marks a generic or repetitive (not specific) event in the context of a distant past time reference.

(50) a. ífè   chì   mé-!ní-sá   mé   lék ḿkpọ́ yí
        people PDEM^pl cpl-INCH-struggle PREP body thing PDEM^sg
        The people would struggle over this thing (but) they

        í-gàk   kpĕ-kọ̀t
        NSP-pass cpl^NEG-able
        would not be able (to mention it).

     b. gwúñ yí   î-rà   í-bọ̀kọ́   ìkpòkò
        boy PDEM^sg 3SG-GEN NSP-receive money
        The boy would receive some money (from the people).

In example (51) *rà* marks a generic event in the context of a future time reference.

(51) mé ìyâkwùt ì-bô-rè ń-sĭ-tùmú òwù ó-rà í-rọ́
PREP tomorrow 3SG-DFUT-be 1SG-CNS-speak 2SG 2SG-GEN NSP-do

ké ó-nọ́
COMP 2SG-hear

Tomorrow it is going to be that whenever I speak, you will do, do you hear?

On the other hand, without a predefined time reference, as in proverbs and expository discourse context, *rà* marks a timeless truth, a generic truth that holds any time, all the time. This is illustrated in (52), a proverb.

(52) útọ́ñ ò-nộ íkộ é-kì-tùmú íkộ m̀gbộ gê î-rà
ear 3SG-hear word CPL-IMPF-speak word time one 3SG-GEN

í-nọ́
NSP-hear

(For) an ear that hears, people only speak once (and) it hears.

4
The Perfect

The perfect is a particularly problematic category. Three views of the perfect are presented in literature. One classifies the perfect as tense because, like tense, it is deictic, relating the time of a situation (E) to a reference time (R/S) during which the state created by the situation is still relevant. Secondly, it does not tell anything about the internal temporal constituency of the situation like aspects do.

Another view classifies the perfect as aspect which has a compositional meaning of tense plus aspect. Since some readings of the perfect seem to require treatment as referring to a state resulting from a previous event, the meaning of the perfect in this instance is not merely tense, but a combination of tense and aspect.

The third view, realizing this compositionality, treats the perfect as a separate category in its own right, neither as tense nor as aspect. I prefer this treatment because treating it purely as tense ignores its aspectual meaning which may be the dominant feature in some contexts. Also treating it purely as aspect ignores its tense meaning which may also be dominant in some contexts.[21]

Apart from the status and types of perfect, some scholars discuss the use of the term "perfect" only for the "present perfect." The present

---

[21]See McCoard (1978) and Anderson (1982) for more detailed discussions of the perfect.

perfect, however, is only one of the possible tenses of the perfect, which may also include past perfect (pluperfect) and future perfect.[22]

4.1 The perfect in Obolo

My data support the viewpoint that there is a grammatical category of perfect in Obolo, and that it is morphologically marked with the morpheme rà/ràbí.[23] As pointed out in §3.4, this morpheme also marks genericity. The two uses of the morpheme are contrasted in section §4.3.

Faraclas (1984a:62) proposes that this morpheme is an optional marker of anterior (past) tense. However, I find no arguments in support of this view of rà. If rà marks anteriority, it does so only to the extent that anteriority is one of the properties of the perfect. As §3.2 shows, anteriority has a zero morphological marking on the verb, with or without a past temporal adverbial.

Also, if rà were an optional anterior morpheme, it would be possible to insert it into all anterior contexts where it was optionally left out, but this is not always so, as example (53) shows. The naturalness of (53a) versus the awkwardness of (53b) is a pragmatic issue.

(53) a. m̀gbọ̀ ò-râ-ràkà ebí òbòlò é-kí-má
time 3sg-REDUP-past DET^pl Obolo cpl-IMPF-like
(in) time(s) past, Obolo people used to like/prefer...

b. *m̀gbọ̀ ò-râ-ràkà ebí òbòlò mî-rà í-kí-má
time 3sg-REDUP-past DET^pl Obolo cpl-RA NSP-IMPF-like
(in) time(s) past, Obolo people have been preferring...

While (53a) simply encodes a past situation, (53b) is very different. The awkwardness of (b) arises from the fact that the use of rà requires a definite reference time point, and m̀gbọ̀ òràràkà '(in) time past' is not definite enough. This requirement is a property of the perfect. Therefore, rà is better analyzed as a marker of the perfect, not an indicator of anteriority.

---

[22]Concerning this argument, Comrie has this to say, "It should be borne in mind that the present perfect (often simply called the perfect) is only one of the possible tenses of the perfect aspect, the one that expresses a relation between present state and the past situation. In other tenses we find, for instance, a past perfect (pluperfect), e.g., *John had eaten the fish*, expressing a relation between a past state and an even earlier situation; and a future perfect, e.g., *John will have eaten the fish*, expressing a relation between a future state and a situation prior to it..." (1976:53).

[23]The forms, rà-, ràbí-, and also ràrí-, bà, bàbí, are idiolectical and dialectical variants of the same morpheme, and they are used interchangeably by Ngo dialect speakers in different towns and villages.

Furthermore, if *rà* were an (optional) anteriority marker, it would occur (whenever it did so) in contexts where anteriority is the dominant feature. But throughout my database, *rà* only occurs in perfect contexts where current relevance is the dominant feature, not mere anteriority. An example of such a context is given in (54) where the time in focus is the moment of speech.

(54) *ìké m̀gbọ̀ kèyí kè èjì mî-ràbí í-kí-tét írîn*
      limit time PDEM SBJ 1pl cpl-PFCT NSP-IMPF-catch fish
      By this time, we would have been catching fish.

A final argument against *rà* as marker of anteriority is a contrast between an anterior sentence with *rà* and one without. Sentence (55) is a simple past question with the nonfuture form (i.e., with no temporal marking) while (56) contains the *rà* morpheme.

(55) *ìrè ífè chà mî-nàñá*
      QUES people DEM^pl cpl-depart
      Did those people depart?

(56) *ìrè ífè chà mî-rà í-nàñá*
      QUES people DEM^pl cpl-RA NSP-depart
      Have those people departed (by now)?

Pragmatically, (55) and (56) do not have the same meaning, the difference between them being that of expectation. In (55) the speaker asks whether or not a certain group of people known to both speaker and hearer did depart. But in (56) the speaker has an expectation that, at the time of asking, the people were to have left already. The relevance of the guests' departure at the time of questioning is present in (56) but absent in (55). Therefore, (56) expresses the perfect, while (55) is a simple anterior sentence.

4.2 The future and past perfect

In Obolo, the perfect also occurs in the context of the future[24] and past tenses and are marked with the same morpheme as the present, i.e.,

---

[24]The future perfect is not often used by speakers of the language. For pragmatic reasons, the past (i.e., nonfuture) perfect in the future is mostly used where one would expect to find the future perfect forms. In this example, therefore, in place of *mê-ràbí* (cpl^FUT-PFCT), *mî-ràbí* (cpl-PFCT) would be used. This would mean: 'By the end of next year we will have already finished building our house' (lit. 'we have finished'). The past perfect in the future is also covered in the schematic representation in (58).

rà/ràbì. Examples (57) and (59) illustrate the future perfect and past perfect, respectively.

(57) òtâ áchà ò-kî-nù èjì mê-ràbí í-námá úwù kìjì
     end year 3SG-IMPF-come 1PL CPL^FUT-PFCT NSP-build house 1PL^POSS

     í-sáñá
     NSP-finish
     (By) the end of next year we will have finished building our house.

Example (57) is represented schematically as in (58).

(58) ---|---|---|--→ Future perfect
       S   E   R

In (58) R stands for áchà ò-kî-nù 'the coming year', a future time reference, and is preceded by the event time, E. The subject prefix on ràbí alternates appropriately to mê- (CPL^FUT) to reflect this futurity.

(59) ìrè î-ràbí í-námá úwù kàñ í-sáñá sǎbùm î-kwù-bé
     QUES 3SG-PFCT NSP-build house 3SG^POSS NSP-finish before 3SG-die-REL
     Had he finished building his house before he died?

Example (59) may be represented schematically as shown in (60).

(60) ---|---|---|--→ Past (i.e., nonfuture) perfect
       E   R   S

In (60) R stands for sǎbùm î-kwù-bé 'before he died', a past time reference, and E occurred before it. In relative tense theory, this would be classified as past in the past, or pluperfect.

4.3 The polysemy of rà

As discussed in §4.2, the morpheme rà has two functions, both temporal. It functions as a marker of genericity as was discussed in §3.4, and it also marks the perfect. There are syntactic and pragmatic indicators that show that the two functions are separate.

First, in a clause chain, where two or more clauses are conjoined with overt conjuctions, the pronominal prefixes on all postconjunction clauses neutralize to the high-toned neutralized subject prefix (NSP) í- in the perfect, but do not neutralize in the generic use. This is illustrated in

The Perfect

(61). (In examples (61)–(62) in this section, (a) is the perfect and (b) is the generic use. The morpheme *rà-* and all postconjunction pronominal prefixes are bolded in the examples.)

(61) a. *gwúñ   yà   î-rà   í-bọ̀kọ̀   ìkpòkò   mè   í-sà*
       boy   DDEM^sg 3SG-PFCT NSP-receive   money   CONJ NSP-take

   í-jé   í-fó
   NSP-walk   NSP-go^home
   The boy has collected some money (and) has walked home with it.

b. *gwúñ   yà   î-rà   í-bọ̀kọ̀   ìkpòkò   mè   ó-sà*
   boy   DDEM^sg 3SG-GEN   3sg-receive money   CONJ 3sg-take

   ó-jè   ó-fò
   3sg-walk   3sg-go^home
   The boy would collect some money (and) would walk home with it.

Secondly, a perfect *rà* clause is independent of any other clauses. But the generic *rà* clause is completely dependent on other clauses, main or subordinate. If subordinate, it may be consequential or conditional. Therefore, if a *rà* clause occurs independently, it is the perfect, not generic. If it is preceded by a consequential or conditional clause, it is generic, not the perfect. These are illustrated in (62).

(62) a. *ìrè   èbí   ìchèn   chà   mî-rà   í-nàñá*
       QUES DET^pl   visitors   DDEM^pl CPL-PFCT NSP-depart
       Have the visitors departed?

b. *èmâ   í-sĭ-ká   úwú-íkpá   mî-rà   í-rié   ínôriè*
   3pl   3pl-CNS-return   school   CPL-GEN   NSP-eat   food
   Whenever they return from school, they would eat.

Thirdly, pragmatically, the perfect *rà* always expresses specific events, never generic. Generic *rà* never expresses specific events. It is used to encode generic, habitual, recurrent events, and timeless truths, and all of these are contexts in which the perfect would never occur. The (a) examples in (61) and (62) encode specific events while the (b) examples in both cases encode recurrent events, with no reference to, or emphasis on, any specific instances of the recurring events.

Apart from being polysemous, the morpheme *rà-* occurs in main clauses, never in subordinate clauses. This similarity may be said to be accidental since there is no syntactic or semantic relationship between the two uses of *rà-*.

5
Aspect

Aspect is defined as "different ways of viewing the internal temporal constituency of a situation" (Comrie 1976:3). Obolo is a language rich in serial verb constructions,[25] and this chapter focuses on the main event expressed by the serial verb construction. Other verbs may take on non-verbal functions, e.g., adverbial, aspectual, and, therefore, the tests for distinguishing aspectual types do not apply to them.

Obolo has three aspectual distinctions: inherent aspect, perfectivity aspect, and phasal aspect. Bybee (1985) notes that inceptives and iteratives, which are phasal aspects in my system, differ from perfectives and imperfectives on the grounds that they are derivational while perfectives and imperfectives are inflectional. In this way, she sets inceptives and iteratives apart from the perfective/imperfective distinction. But since she recognizes only one distinction, i.e., perfective/imperfective, it follows that the inceptive and iterative, though aspects, are left unclassified in Bybee's system.

In Obolo there are two criteria for recognizing the three aspectual distinctions. One is the locus of influence of the different types of aspects. While inherent and phasal aspects are realized at the lexical level, perfectivity aspect is realized at the grammatical level. Also, while inherent aspect applies to the whole event, phasal aspects apply to phases and subphases of events. The second criterion is that these three distinctions can co-occur morphologically in a single verbal expression. This co-occurrence is discussed in §§5.6–5.8.

---

[25]In a serial verb construction, more than one verb occurs serially to express one major event.

Phasal aspect includes aspectual encodings such as inceptive, completive, durative, iterative, immediative, and inchoative, all of which, in one way or the other, involve phases or subphases of situations.[26] Perfectivity in Obolo includes perfective and imperfective, while inherent aspect includes states, activities, semelfactives, accomplishments, and achievements.

5.1 Perfectivity aspect

In Obolo, verbs are either imperfective (marked with *kî*) or perfective (unmarked). The perfective aspect in Obolo is a default classification. Given the binary perfectivity system that I have adopted, since the imperfective is always marked, it follows that the absence of any imperfective marking indicates the perfective. Therefore, all main verbs with zero aspectual morphological marking are perfective.[27] The totality view of perfectivity is not a temporal notion since perfectives may occur with states and activities which have no terminal points. Rather, it is a dimension of communicative packaging for presentation in the course of discourse—either as a wrapped-up whole (perfective), or unfolded to make its internal structure accessible (imperfective). Perfective looks at the situation from outside, without distinguishing any of its internal structure, while imperfective looks at the situation from inside, and is crucially concerned with the internal temporal constituency of the situation. Example (63) illustrates a state with perfective interpretation and (64) an activity with perfective interpretation. The situation in both (63) and (64) is presented as a whole without concern for its internal structure.

(63) *ífè   chà   árâñ   ó-kúp   mé   ísí*
      people DDEM^pl oil   3sg-stay PREP front
      There was oil in front of those people.

---

[26]Because the scope of the durative and the iterative includes the entire event, they do not readily appear to relate to phases. However, seen from within the event, they tell something about the internal constituency of the whole event, including phases. For instance, the iterative expresses that each phase of the event is a repetition of the others. Also, the durative, which expresses that the event is a long drawn out one, includes all the phases or subphases of the event in its scope. Because of the presence of phases or subphases of the event in their meanings, they are different from the perfectivity aspects which do not focus on phases of the event. Therefore, they are best classified as phasal aspects.

[27]Main verb here refers to a verb that constitutes the head of the verb phrase whether or not the verb phrase is a serial verb construction.

Aspect

(64) *gwúñ yà   ó-!nê-nĭ-gọ̀ọ́k*
child DDEM^sg 3SG-REDUP-INC-follow
(Then) the boy followed (it).

Other characteristics of the totality view of perfectivity, include: (1) statives may be perfective regardless of time reference; (2) future situations can be perfective freely without reference to other situations; and (3) present situations can also be perfective. Obolo iteratives and inchoatives are treated under a separate category since the perfective and imperfective co-occur with inchoatives and iteratives in the same way as they co-occur with inherent aspects. Unlike inherent aspect which operates at the lexical level and carries no overt marking, perfectivity aspect operates at the grammatical or discourse level, and is marked by inflectional morphology in Obolo.

On the basis of markedness, there are three splits in the perfectivity aspect system in the language. There is, first, a perfective/imperfective split, then there is a habitual/nonhabitual split, and finally, a progressive/continuous split. The habitual carries the simplest imperfective marking *ki*, while the progressive and continuous carry extra periphrastic marking along with *ki*. This three-way split is represented in (65).

(65)   Obolo perfectivity aspect

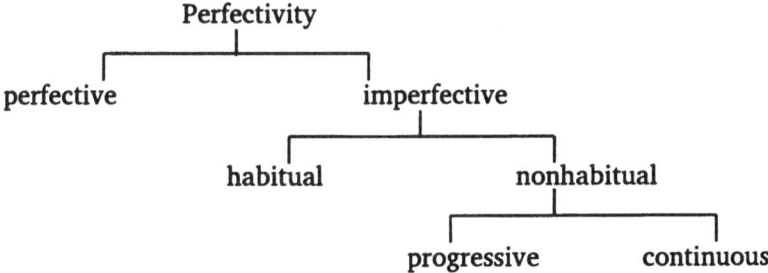

The discussion in the rest of this section begins with the imperfective because, being the marked member of the opposition, its properties are easily observable in terms of form and function. The perfective, the unmarked member, is discussed after the imperfective.

5.1.1 Imperfective aspect

As shown in (65), the Obolo imperfective finds expression in habitual, progressive, and continuous subcategories. Both progressive and continuous are grouped under the nonhabitual node. The imperfective can be formed from any verb by the prefixation of the inflectional morpheme *ki* next to the verb root. The position of this morpheme relative to the verb stem follows the pattern found in other languages where the aspect marker occurs closest to the verb root, in contrast with categories such as tense and mood which tend to occur farther away fom the verb root. The morpheme *ki* occurs in all expressions of habituality, continuity, and progressivity, thus marking imperfectivity in Obolo.

The habitual aspect. Semantically, the habitual expresses a situation that obtains consistently for a long time, as illustrated in (66). It is marked by the imperfective marker *ki*. Example (66a) below is a generic habitual situation, while (66b) is a time-based habitual situation.

(66) a. ǹsàbọ́n   úwù-íkpá   é-kí-jé   èsêsé
         children school   cpl-IMPF-behave different
         School children habitually behave differently.

    b. ń-kí-sí   m̀bọ́m   úsèn   géèlék
       1sg-IMPF-go fishing day   every
       I go fishing every day.

Progressive aspect. That an event is progressive prototypically implies that the event is in process at the reference time. This situation is expressed with a combination of the existential locative morpheme *gâ* (sg) or *bâ* (pl),[28] an unbound auxiliary, and the imperfective affix *kí* with high tone, coupled with a special pronominal prefix paradigm (ǹ- 1sg, ò- 2/3sg, mê- all pl). Also, the verb stem retains its basic tone, i.e., high for high tone verbs and low for low tone verbs. The paradigm of progressive marking is given in (67). The parentheses indicate that the locative, *gâ/bâ*, is optional with the 3sg and all plural persons.

(67)   Paradigm of the progressive markers

       -gâ   ǹ-kí-   (fast speech -gá-!kí-)   1sg
       -gâ   ò-kí-   (fast speech -gá-!kí-)   2sg
       (-gâ)   ò-kí-   3sg
       (-bâ)   mê-kí-   (fast speech -mé-!kí-)   all pl

---

[28]The morpheme *gâ* (actually *gwâ*)/ *bâ* is a very uncommon type of existential locative verb. Its only other use is in greetings such as *òwù ò-gwâ* 'are you (sg) there', *ènyì è-bâ* 'are you (pl) there'. Its rarity suggests that it is possibly a remnant of a former class system. To the extent that these locative verbs do not alternate for tense, aspect, mood, and focus for which all verbs prototypically alternate, they have become suppletive and have grammaticized to become a progressive aspect marker. It is labelled progressive (locative) marker (PLOC) in the examples.

Aspect

The use of the locative to mark progressive aspect is common in many languages. Examples illustrating the progressive are given in (68) with the progressive (locative) marker (PLOC) *gâ* and (69) without *gâ*.

(68) ògwú gwúñ ó-!ní-bé ké ọ̀mọ̀ ò-gâ ò-kí-rié
DET^sg child 3SG-INC-say COMP 3SG 3SG-PLOC 3SG-IMPF-eat
Her child said that he was eating.

(69) mé àtíkộ òbòlò ò-kí-bóló
PREP truth Obolo 3SG-IMPF-wake^up
Truly, Obolo is waking up!

Even though the default temporal reference for the progressive, which may be marked by *gâ/bâ* and/or *kí*, is the present time, i.e., the moment of speech, as in example (69), nevertheless the morphemes *gâ/bâ* also co-occur with past or future adverbials or temporal clauses to mark past or future events in process, as illustrated in (70) and (71). In (70), the temporal clause, 'when s/he came', clearly refers to a past event that is known to both interlocutors in the speech situation, and in (7), the clause, 'when s/he will come' is clearly marked for futurity. But the morpheme -*gâ* still co-occurs with both of them and is, therefore, not a present-tense marker.

(70) m̀gbọ̀ î-nù-bè èmì ñ-gá-!kí-kén múñ
time 3SG-come-REL 1SG 1SG-PLOC-IMPF-bathe water
When s/he came, I (was) bathing.

(71) m̀gbọ̀ ì-bô-nù èmì ñ-gá-!kí-kén múñ
time 3SG-IFUT-come 1SG 1SG-PLOC-IMPF-bathe water
At the time s/he will come, I (shall be) bathing.

Continuous aspect. The continuous aspect is optionally marked periphrastically using the verb *kpọ́/kpọ́kpộ*[29] 'look' in a serial verb construction with *kí* affixed to the main verb stem. This is exemplified in (72), which is taken from the Orphan story. The absence of the special pronominal prefix paradigm (see (67)) indicates that (72) does not exemplify the progressive.

(72) *í-kpộkpọ̀* í-kí-sìsáak ògwú énêrièèñ
3SG-look NSP-IMPF-disturb DET^sg man
She kept on disturbing the man.

---

[29] The serial verb *kpọ/kpọkpọ* may also mark persistence, which is a modal meaning.

Elsewhere in my database, continuous meaning is expressed with *kí* alone, without *kpọ́/kpọ́kpộ*. This type of continuous aspect is exemplified in (73) where the boy began to sing and continued to sing for some time, hence the use of *kí*.

(73) ìkéyà   ké   î-nì-bènè   ókwà   í-kí-kọ́t
     that^way COMP 3sg-INC-begin   song   NSP-IMPF-sing
     So he began singing a song.

5.1.2 Perfective aspect

As discussed above, all main verbs with zero aspectual morphological marking (i.e., not marked with *ki*) are perfective. Perfective verbs have the following characteristics: They present the event as a wrapped-up whole. They include arbitrary end points with activities, natural end points with accomplishments, no end point with states, and they focus on the single-phase event in semelfactives and achievements. They carry perfective meaning in any time reference, future or nonfuture. Examples of the perfective aspect are given in (74) to (78).

In example (74), a nonfuture stative situation, the perfective does not indicate any end point. The situation is viewed from the outside as a single whole, without any regard for the internal structure, which states do not have.

(74) ì-rè   ḿkpọ́ yí   î-gbĕ   èmì   yê
     3sg-be   thing PDEM^sg   3sg-suit   1sg   QUES
     Does this thing suit me?

In (75), which is an immediate future accomplishment, the perfective situation, viewed as a whole, includes a natural end point.

(75) *ké   ọ̀mộ   mô-nĭ-tàp   gwúñ   kàñ   mé   úwù-íkpá*
     COMP   3sg   FUT-INC-put   child   3sg^POSS   PREP   school
     that he was going to put his child into school.

In (76), a generic tense-neutral activity, the perfective situation which is also viewed as a whole, implies an arbitrary end point.

(76) *mè è-tákà   ágòk*
     3sg cpl-chew   chewing^stick
     They would chew the chewing stick.

Aspect

In (77), a generic tense-neutral achievement, the perfective situation includes a natural end point.

(77) mè è-mûñ lék ògbògbò íkọ́t mé èmèn
CONJ cpl-see body much crayfish PREP inside
And (they) would spot a lot of crayfish inside (the trap).

Finally, in (78), a conditional nonfuture semelfactive situation, the perfective focuses on the single-phased event.

(78) íré gwúñ î-kpám chiéèñ
COND child 3sg-blink eye
if the child blinked his/her eyes

5.1.3 Distribution of the perfectivity aspect

The imperfective knows no constraints. It co-occurs with all tenses in the indicative mood. It occurs cross-modally with the imperative, hortative, and the infinitive, as exemplified in (79). It also co-occurs with inherent and phasal aspects discussed later.

(79) Cross-modal distribution of the imperfective

Indicative	simple future		môkírié	's/he will be eating'
	definite future		ìbôkírié	's/he will be eating'
	immediate future		mônìkírié	's/he is about to be eating'
	nonfuture		íkìriè	's/he eats' (used to be eating)
Conditional			mókírié	'if s/he would be eating'
Infinitive			íkêkírié	'to be eating' (ki is reduplicated in the infinitive)
Imperative	sg		kírié	'(2sg) be eating'
	pl		ìkìrié	'(2pl) be eating'
Hortative:	sg		íkírié	'let him/her be eating'
	pl		ékérié	'let them/us be eating'

In the same way, the perfective aspect also occurs in all moods. Removal of *kí* from the chart in (79) gives the cross-modal forms of the perfective as shown in (80).

(80) Cross-modal distribution of the perfective

Indicative	simple future	*môriè*	's/he will eat'
	definite future	*ìbôriè*	's/he is going to eat'
	immediate future	*mônǐrié*	's/he is about to eat'
	nonfuture	*îriè*	's/he ate'
Conditional		*môrié*	'if s/he would eat'
Infinitive		*írêriè*	'to eat'
Imperative	sg	*riê*	'(2sg) eat'
	pl	*ìriê*	'(2pl) eat'
Hortative	sg	*íriê*	'let him/her eat'
	pl	*ériê*	'let them/us eat'

5.2 Inherent aspect

This lexical aspect first proposed by Vendler (1957) consists of four classes of verbs: states, activities, accomplishments, and achievements. It was expanded by Smith (1991) to include semelfactives (punctual activities). The temporal properties by which these subtypes of the inherent aspect are analyzed are: dynamic/nondynamic or static, durative/nondurative (punctual or instantaneous), and telic/atelic (i.e., bounded/unbounded). Dynamicity has to do with whether or not the event in question involves change of state, i.e., whether or not one phase of the event is different from the other. The durative/nondurative distinction has to do with whether the duration of the event occupies a span of time, or is punctual. Telicity has to do with whether or not the event in question has a natural terminal point, either overtly stated or implied. If it does, then it is said to be bounded or telic, but if it does not, then it is said to be unbounded or atelic. A slightly amended version of Lee's diagram (1991:34) is given in (81) to show these properties diagramatically.

Aspect

(81) Inherent aspect (adapted from Lee 1991:34)

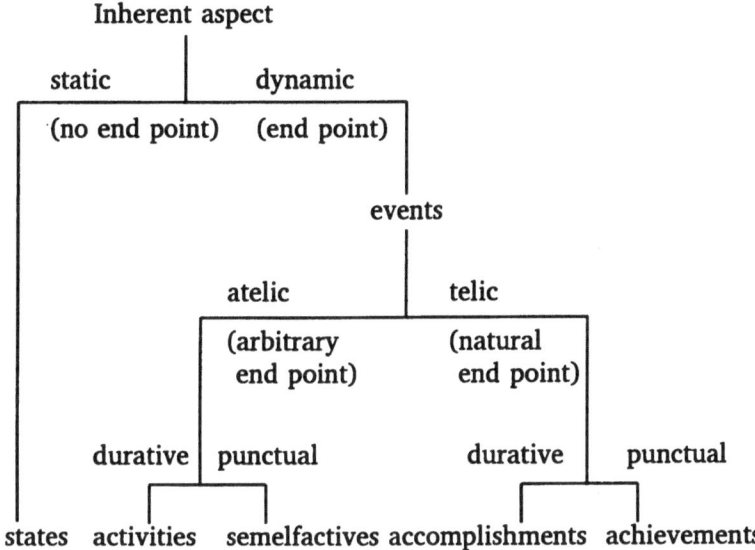

In its expression, inherent aspect is purely semantic, without any morphological marking, as is borne out in my database. In this way it is different from the other types of aspect which have some sort of morphological marking. The five subtypes are discussed next in the order of states, activities, semelfactives, accomplishments, and achievements.

States. Intrinsic state verbs[30] are inherently not dynamic (i.e., they do not involve change of state) and they are nonphasal, i.e., since they do not involve a change of state, each phase of a stative situation is the same as all other phases. States have no internal structure, are nondynamic, nonvolitional, not subject to control, and do not require any energy to keep going. By extension, therefore, they are nonagentive.

The intrinsically stative verbs in my database are classified into six different categories: existential, attributive,[31] possessive, perceptive, cognitive, and affective. These are listed in (82) along with some of the verbs that index them.

---

[30]The states discussed here are intrinsic states, and are purely lexical. Derived stative constructions and idiomatic statives formed from nonstates, as well as verbless existential stative constructions are excluded.

[31]The abundant presence of the attributive statives may be said to compensate for, or to be the cause of, the restriction on the number of true adjectives, thus making adjectives a rather closed category in the language.

(82) existential kúp   'stay, remain'
                  rê   'be'
     attributive wâ   'be many, much, plenty'
                  tóp   'be delicious, pleasing'
                  jọ́ñọ̀   'be long, distant'
     possessive   káañ   'have, possess'
     perceptive   múñ   'see (not spot)'
                  nộ   'hear'
     cognitive   riọ̀ọ́ñ 'know'
                  chièék 'believe, agree'
     affective   mâ   'like, love'
                  chằ   'hate, dislike'

Examples illustrating intrinsic attributive and cognitive stative verbs are given in (83) and (84). The verbs in these examples are both nonvolitional. For instance, in (83), once the names become pleasing to the parents' ears, they continue to remain so. The parents do not need to expend any energy to keep the names pleasing to their ears. The concept of the names being pleasing to their ears is not a process, nor does it involve any change of states. Therefore, it is not phasal, and not dynamic.

(83) íré míjè èriéeñ yà ó-*tóp*-bé émâ mé ùtọ́ñ
     but because name DEM^sg 3sg-pleasing-REL 3pl PREP ear
     but because the name is pleasing to their ears

(84) mé m̀gbọ̀ yà ówùwà énê mê-*riọ̀ọ́ñ* òwù ísí
     PREP time DEM^sg many people cpl-know 2sg face
     At that time, many people will know you.

Activities. Activities are dynamic, durative, and atelic. They usually have no goals, and no culmination or natural end point. Therefore, termination here means cessation of activity. Further, all activities are volitional, subject to control, and need energy to keep going and are, therefore, agentive. Some intrinsic activity verbs observed in my database are listed in (85).

(85) kọ́t   'sing'   kwọ̀kộ 'peel, scrape' tákà 'chew'
     bê   'say'   dò   'ask'   lákà 'lick'
     tùmû 'speak'   tàbâ 'pull'   kpằ   'tell'
     gọ̀ọ́k 'follow'   sî   'go'   sùlû 'beat'
     jề   'walk'   kpọ̀   'look'   wèék 'look for'
     gbộ   'clear (bush)' wùlû 'fly'   kékè 'stand'
     rọ̀   'do'   tô   'cry'   lăp   'chase off'
     tíík 'abuse'   bàlâ 'decorate'   bọ́m   'fish'

Aspect 45

Examples of activities are given in (86) to (88). In these examples, the verbs are volitional, durative, and do not imply any natural terminal points. Only the subjects themselves can terminate the actions. They all involve change of state and are phasal. For instance, saying something in (87) involves multiple activities with the mouth, and looking for money in (88) involves many activities with the whole body, each of these activities being a phase in the course of the overall event. Looking for money takes a much longer time than saying something, yet they are both activities.

(86) úkó ènyì é-kí-gbộ-*gbọ̀*   yê
 farm 2pl cpl-IMPF-REDUP-weed QUES
 How are you (pl) weeding the farm?

(87) èbí árâñ é-!nê-nǐ-*bé*
 DET^pl oil cpl-REDUP-INC-say
 Then the oil (eaters) said

(88) mè **wèék**   ìkpòkò sọ̀kọ́   lék
 CONJ 2sg^IMP^look^for money 2sg^IMP^add body
 and look for money to add to it

Semelfactives. Semelfactives are similar to activities in that they are atelic, dynamic, volitional, and consequently, agentive. But on the other hand, unlike activities, semelfactives are instantaneous. It is possible for any of these events to be said to go on for a long time. But durativity with respect to semelfactives involves repetitions of the same event rather than that the event has a long span. Some semelfactives are listed in (89).

(89) kpám 'blink (of eyes), crackle (of fire)'
 tóbò 'hit (resultative form)'
 kọ̀lộ 'cough'
 kwák 'clap (of hands)'
 gŏn 'knock, hit with a hammer'

Examples illustrating the semelfactive are given in (90) and (91). One of the meanings of (90) is that the action of clapping was done only once. The durativity indicated by the morpheme kí in (91) implies that the clapping action was being repeated.

(90) m̀gbọ̀ yà   ǹté î-kwàk úbọ́k
 time DDEM^sg Nte 3sg-clap hand
 At that time, Nte clapped (his) hands.

(91) m̀gbọ̀ yà   ǹté ò-kí-kwák   úbọ́k
    time DDEM^sg Nte 3sg-IMPF-clap hand
    At that time, Nte was clapping (his) hands.

Accomplishments. Accomplishments are dynamic, durative, and telic events, and they result in change of state. They are similar to activities in that they are dynamic and durative, but different in that they are telic while activities are atelic. Like semefactives, accomplishments are dynamic, but while semelfactives are atelic, and punctual, accomplishments are telic and durative.

Two kinds of accomplishments were observed in my database: intrinsic and derived accomplishments. While the intrinsic ones are single verbs with intrinsic accomplishment properties, derived accomplishments consist of activity verbs plus "bounders" (Bybee 1985). These bounders consist of another verb placed in series with the first verb to indicate completion, complement, resultative, or goal; the presence of a direct object which marks termination of the event in question; or a relative clause suffixal morpheme -*be,* which indicates completion or termination. Relativization carries the implication that the event in the clause is either completed or terminated. These bounders transform intrinsic atelic activity verbs into telic accomplishment verbs.

Intrinsic accomplishment verbs observed in my database are listed in (92). Each of these verbs, with or without bounders, implies a natural terminal point and results in a change of state, as (93) and (94) illustrate.

(92) tặp   'put'   bọ̀kộ   'receive'   gwén   'call, name'
      nyì̀   'give'   tét   'catch'   chít   'cover, close'
      mọ̀nộ   'take'   tô   'put down'   tòóń   'place on'
      gwọ̀   'scoop'   bén   'carry'   nyám   'sell'
      kpùlû 'gather'   bénè   'lift'   tô   'measure, order'
      sóók   'shoot'   fô   'go home'   tééń   'pick (many things)'
      kpáñ   'kill'   kà̀   'return'   tô   'cast (a line)'

In (93), the action of lifting up the fish trap out of the water requires a long time span, but it has a definite end point and results in a change of state. So also is the taking of the child to the fishing port in (94). Both are dynamic actions.

(93) mî-rà   í-ní-béné
    cpl-GEN NSP-INCH-lift
    Then they would lift (the fish trap out of the water).

(94) mî-rà í-**mọ̀nọ́** gwúñ yà
cpl-PERF NSP-take child DDEM^sg
They would take the child.

In both examples, without any bounders, the intrinsic accomplishment verbs by themselves imply durativity, telicity, and dynamicity. But this is not the case with derived accomplishment verbs. Derived accomplishments observed in my database, showing the activity verbs and bounders, are given in (95). The nature of the bounders are given in parentheses beside each one. Examples illustrating the telicization effect of the bounders on the atelic activity verbs are given in (96) and (97). Example (96) contains an unbounded atelic activity verb, while (97) contains the same activity verb, but this time, bounded, and thus transformed into an accomplishment verb.

(95) | Activity verb | | Bounder | | Nature of bounder |
|---|---|---|---|---|
| kwééñ | 'learn' | sáñà | 'finish' | (COMPLETION) |
| riê | 'eat' | ínôriè íkàkwùñ | 'supper' | (DIRECT OBJECT) |
| rọ̀ | 'do, make' | ínyí òwù òriọ̀ọ̀ñ | 'so that you know' | (COMPLEMENT) |
| súlû | 'beat' | kpáñ | 'kill' | (RESULTATIVE) |
| lìbî | 'run' | sìbî | 'come out' | (GOAL) |
| kwọ̀kọ́ | 'catch' | -bé | (REL) | (relative clause here indicates COMPLETION) |

(96) ké   ògwú íjêjèèñ mô-sùlù   gwúñ kìbàñ
COMPL DET^sg teacher 3sg^FUT-beat child 3pl^POSS
that the teacher would beat their child

(97) ké   ògwú íjêjèèñ mô-sùlù   gwúñ kìbàñ   í-kpáñ
COMP DET^sg teacher 3sg^FUT-beat child 3pl^POSS NSP-kill
that the teacher would beat their child to death

Achievements. Achievements are dynamic, punctual, and telic events which result in change of state. Achievement verbs have all the properties of accomplishment verbs, except that they are punctual, while accomplishment verbs are durative. Intrinsic achievement verbs observed in my database are listed in (98).

(98) bólò 'wake up'   sìbî 'go/come out, quit'
     múñ 'see (spot)'   ràkâ 'pass'
     níñ 'enter'   rê 'reach, arrive'
     sò̩ 'become right (quantity)' nàñâ 'depart'
     tâ 'finish, end'   bénè 'begin'

Schematically, an achievement verb consists of a single phase which constitutes a change of state. For instance, when a glass breaks, as illustrated in (99), certain events may lead up to the point of breaking e.g., Ene may have been doing something with the glass. But the breaking is a single phase, and by itself, constitutes the change of state in the condition of the glass. Also in (100), the expending of the last bit of money, a single phase, constitutes a change of state.

(99) énê î-bùm   ékpéñ
     Ene 3sg-break glass
     Ene broke the glass.

(100) ìkpòkò î-tà
      money 3sg-finish
      The money is finished.

5.3 Phasal aspect

This third type of aspect is concerned with subevents or phases/subphases of the overall event. The members of the phasal aspect group include: inceptive, completive, durative, iterative, immediative, and inchoative. The members fall into three groups of two each, based on what phase of the situation they focus on. The inceptive and completive focus on endpoints. While the inceptive focuses on the beginning point, the completive focuses on the final point. The durative and iterative focus on the middle phase. While the durative describes the situation as a long, drawn-out event, the iterative describes the situation as consisting of several repetitions of the same mini-event. Immediative and inchoative focus on the boundary between two consecutive situations. While immediative signals the absence of a temporal gap between the two situations, the inchoative signals the fact that there has been a change of situation, without indicating precisely when the change took place. While the first four are intra-event, because they focus on phases within the same situation, the last two are inter-event, because they focus on the boundary between two situations. These are shown schematically in (101).

Aspect 49

(101) Obolo phasal aspect

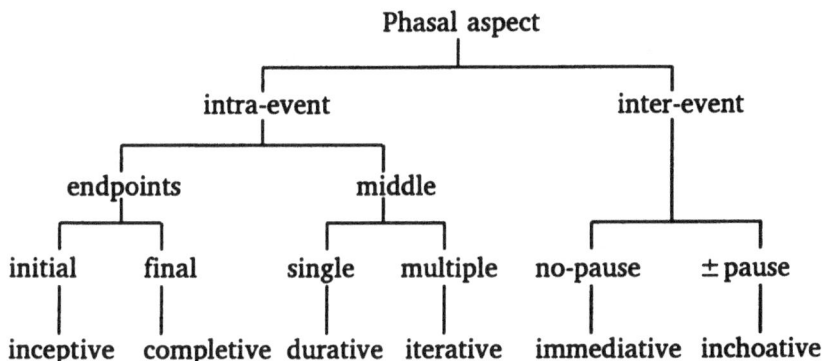

The different subtypes of phasal aspect are discussed below in the order inceptive, completive, durative, iterative, immediative, and inchoative.

Inceptive. I define the inceptive as an ingressive aspect which indicates the entry into a situation. It is different from the inchoative which indicates the coming about of a situation. When it is necessary to highlight the beginning of an event, the inceptive is marked periphrastically by means of the verb *bénè* 'begin' in a serial verb construction. This is exemplified in (102). In this example, the casting of the net is a long process, and it is also repeated several times during the course of fishing. But it is the beginning of the the process, and by implication, the beginning of the series of net-casting which will be done during this fishing trip, that is signalled. The durativity of the process is indicated by the use of the imperfective morpheme *kí.*

(102) ènyì mê-!bê-**bènè**   í-kí-tó   ńjìn
      2pl cpl^FUT-REDUP-begin NSP-IMPF-cast net
      You (pl) will begin to cast the net.

The inceptive does not only co-occur with situations whose processual nature is overtly indicated by means of the imperfective morpheme *kí.* It also occurs without *kí,* where the situation is naturally understood to be a long process, as illustrated in (103), which is another way of expressing the example in (102).

(103) ènyì mê-**bènè**   í-tó   ńjìn
      2pl cpl^FUT-begin NSP-cast net
      You (pl) will begin to cast the net.

Completive. The completive aspect is used when it is necessary to indicate completion of an event. In a sequential context where it is necessary to include the end point of an activity, a serial verb bounder, *sáñà* 'finish', *ràká* 'pass', or *kĕm* 'be just enough', is used to indicate completion. This is illustrated in (104) to (106). In (104), the completion of the process of putting the net into the boat is signalled.

(104) ènyì í-sĭ-tàp ńjĭn í-**sáñá** mé újí
 2pl cpl-cns-put net nsp-finish prep canoe
 when you (pl) finish putting the net into the boat

Example (105) expresses the completion of the funeral process before the interlocutor's letter arrived.

(105) mî-fùúñ í-**ràká** săbùm
 cpl-bury nsp-pass before
 they already finished burying him before...

In (106), the concern is with reaching the right stage in the tide, whether flow or ebb tide. The right stage has to be reached before the fishing can begin.

(106) múñ í-sĭ-báák í-**kèm** mè ì-rè í-sĭ-tá í-**kèm**
 water 3sg-cns-flow nsp-enough conj 3sg-be 3sg-cns-ebb nsp-enough
 When the flow tide or ebb tide is just right

Durative. The distinction between imperfectivity and durativity according to Comrie (1976:41), is that imperfectivity means viewing a situation with regard to its internal structure, and durativity refers to the fact that the given situation lasts for a certain period of time. Punctuality does not necessarily denote perfectivity, neither does durativity necessarily denote imperfectivity.

In Obolo, apart from durativity that is inherent in states and activities at the lexical level, and in the imperfective aspect at the grammatical level, there are also times when it is necessary to overtly express durativity. This type of durativity is indicated either by repetition of the verb or by a verbal particle, a type of prepositional conjunction *mégê/àbáyàgê* 'until'.

The number of possible repetitions of the verb does not seem to have much restriction. Of the two occurrences in my database, one, which is given in (107), contains three repetitions, while the other, which is given in (108), has four repetitions of the verb. Durativity by repetition only seems to occur in oral texts. Children are known to continue repeating the verb until they are out of breath, to indicate long duration.

(107) mè í-sà   í-jé   *í-jé*   *í-jé*   *í-jé*
CONJ NSP-take NSP-walk NSP-walk NSP-walk NSP-walk
and he walked (off) with it (and) walked (and) walked (and) walked

(108) ékìrìkà   í-sĭ-wút   *í-wút*   *í-wút*   *í-wút*   *í-wút*
harmattan NSP-CNS-blow NSP-blow NSP-blow NSP-blow NSP-blow
when the harmattan blows and blows and blows for a long time

The preposition, *mégê/àbáyàgê* 'until', functions like a bounder to make an unbounded activity verb into a telic situation. But it not only indicates telicity, it also carries a durative meaning which indicates that the activity lasts for a long time. This way of encoding durativity is exemplified in (109). To indicate a very long duration by this means, people tend to make the last vowel as long as it can possibly go.

(109) ìkéyà   ké   î-nì-sà   àchá yà   í-jé   **àbáyàgê**
like^that COMP 3sg-INC-take hoe DDEM^sg NSP-walk until
in that way he took off with the hoe (and) walked until

Iterative. Iterativity is the repetition of a situation or the successive occurrence of several instances of the given situation. In Obolo, it is marked both morphologically and periphrastically. The morphological marking is inflectional. It consists of the reduplication of the first syllable of the verb stem, and the assigning of a low tone to the reduplicated syllable. Iterativity by reduplication of verb stem is exemplified in (110). This way of marking the iterative is rare, and is no longer productive in the language.

(110) **î-fú-fǫ́n**   ìkpòkò   í-kàná   érè
3sg-REDUP-borrow money NSP-turn^round place
He (repeatedly) borrowed money all over the place.

Periphrastically, the iterative is indicated by means of two serial verbs, *kpǫ́k* 'untie' and *yákà* 'turn',[32] in a serial verb construction. Examples illustrating these two verbs are given in (111) and (112), respectively.

(111) í-yâ-**yàkà**   í-ní-kí-kǫ́t
3sg-REDUP-ITER NSP-INC-IMPF-sing
Then he continued to sing again.

---

[32]The morpheme *yákà* is a multipurpose morpheme. Apart from indicating iteratives and nonsequential inchoative, it also indicates other meanings such as 'again' (iteration of same event) and 'also' (list of nonsimilar events).

(112) í-kpộ-**kpọ̀k**   í-bén   í-wùlú
3sg-REDUP-ITER NSP-carry NSP-fly
when it flew away again

Sometimes these two verbs, *yákà* and *kpọ́k*, may co-occur in the same construction where *yákà* will indicate inchoativity while *kpọ́k* indicates iterativity. This is illustrated in (113).

(113) mè   í-yáká   í-kpọ́k   í-bén   í-wùlú
CONJ NSP-INCH NSP-ITER NSP-carry NSP-fly
and it flew away again (unexpectedly)

Immediative. I use the term "immediative" to indicate absence of a pause or a temporal gap between two consecutive events in a sequence. It signals that the first event is immediately followed by the second one without any pause. In this way, it implies completedness of the event in question and the inception of the next event.

To mark immediative, the preceding verb is repeated and its first syllable is reduplicated and assigned a falling tone. In a serial verb construction, where a main verb is preceded by a modifying verb, the modifying verb is the one that undergoes the reduplication. It differs from other reduplications by the fact that it requires the overt statement of the previous verb. Immediative provides temporal connection in a sequence of events in the discourse. It is exemplified here in (114) where the iterative serial verb, a modifying verb, is marked for immediative.

(114) mè   í-yáká   í-kpọ́k   í-bén   í-wùlú
and NSP-INC NSP-ITER NSP-carry NSP-fly
and flew off again.

í-kpộ-**kpọ̀k**   í-bén   í-wùlú gwùn̄ yà   ó-!kê-kĭ-kọ́t
3sg-REDUP-ITER NSP-carry NSP-fly child DDEMˆsg 3sg-REDUP-IMPF-sing
As soon as it flew off again, the boy (began and continued) to sing.

Inchoative. The term "inchoative" is sometimes used to indicate an ingressive meaning, i.e., beginning of an event or a change of state or state-after-change. I use the second meaning of the term inchoative here, i.e., the coming about of a situation that was not present before or expected. It indicates that there has been a change in the state of affairs.

The inchoative is indicated both morphologically and periphrastically. The morphological encoding is done by means of the affix, *ní-*, which is the grammaticized form of the verb *nǎ/nú* 'come'. This is exemplified in

(115). To illustrate the inchoative meaning here, the same example is given in (116) without *ní-*. In (115), there is an indication that the situation has been different before the statement. This is indicated in the English gloss by the adverb 'now'. But in (116), there is no such meaning.

(115) ì-*ní-kí-sí*   m̀bóm̧   írî̧n̄
       3SG-INCH-IMPF-go occupation fish
       He now fishes (for a living).

(116) ì-*kí-sí*   m̀bóm̧   írî̧n̄
       3SG-IMPF-go occupation fish
       He fishes (for a living).

The periphrastic encoding of the inchoative meaning is done by means of the multifunctional verb, *yákà* 'turn', in a serial verb construction. In terms of grammaticization, though both *-ní-* and *yákà* layer as inchoative markers, both have become specialized. While *ní-* indicates sequence, *yákà* indicates nonsequence. Since negation is nonsequential, *yákà*, not *ní-*, is used in negative expressions as the inchoative marker. This is exemplified in (117). To illustrate the inchoative meaning, the same example is given in (118), without *yákà*. The meaning of 'anymore' which is present in (117) to indicate contrast with a previous situation, is not present in (118).

(117) *kpĕ-yáká*   í-*nyí*   ǫ́mǫ̂   m̄kpǫ́ géègè
       cpl^NEG-INC NSP-give 3SG thing any
       They didn't give him anything anymore.

(118) *kpĕ-nyí*   ǫ́mǫ̂   m̄kpǫ́ géègè
       cpl^NEG-give 3SG thing any
       They didn't give him anything.

However, *yákà* as an inchoative marker is found not only in negative expressions but also in affirmative expressions where sequentiality is not an issue. The distribution of *-ní-* and the affirmative use of *yákà* in two sample texts in my database are given in (119).

(119) Distribution of *-ní-* and affirmative *yákà*

Text	-ní-		yákà	
	Number	%	Number	%
WB	30	94%	0	0%
PROGS	2	6%	4	100%
Total	32	100%	4	100%

The table in (119) reveals that the choice between -*ní-* and *yákà* is clearly discourse motivated. The difference between these two texts is that one (WB) is a narrative text, and the other (PROGS) is not a narrative text. Narratives call for sequentiality of events. The WB narrative text calls for sequentiality of events, so the -*ní-* inchoative is employed in it to indicate this sequentiality. In this text, the *yákà* inchoative only occurs in negative expressions where the -*ní-* inchoative cannot occur. The PROGS text is a non-narrative text, an expository compare-and-contrast discourse that describes progress in Obolo country by comparing past and present situations. Therefore, it does not require sequentiality of events. So inchoative verbs in this text, both affirmative and negative, are marked by *yákà* 'turn'. The only exceptions are the two occurrences of -*ní-*, shown in (119), which are found in an embedded narrative in the comparison.

An example of *yákà* as an affirmative inchoative marker is given in (120) which is taken from the nonnarrative PROGS text.

(120) ówùwà énê   mé   ówùwà ámà   mé   chérékèyí e-**yáká**
many people PREP many town PREP today cpl-INC

í-kí-sà   àlàlá
NSP-IMPF-take zinc
Today, many people in many towns are using (roofing) zinc (which they never did before).

Without the inchoative marker, no contrast is indicated. This is illustrated in (121), using the same example.

(121) ówùwà énê   mé   ówùwà ámà   mé   chérékèyí é-kí-sà
many people PREP many town PREP today cpl-IMPF-take

àlàlá
zinc
Today, many people in many towns are using (roofing) zinc.

When the two markers, *yákà* and -*ní-* co-occur, *yákà* indicates iterativity while -*ní-* indicates inchoativity, as illustrated in (122). In this example, the use of the two markers together indicates a resumption of an activity, which was previously terminated.

(122) í-yâ-**yàkà**   í-**ní**-kí-kọ́t
3sg-REDUP-ITER NSP-INC-IMPF-sing
Then he continued to sing again. (lit. He turned back to singing, which he wasn't doing before.)

5.4 Co-occurrence of the different types of aspect

Co-occurrence of the different types of aspect is one of the two criteria upon which I have based the taxonomy of aspect types in Obolo. If two types of aspect co-occur in one verbal expression, especially if they are each marked morphologically on the same verb, it follows that they belong to two different aspectual types. For instance, if an inchoative co-occurs with an imperfective in an activity verb, as illustrated in (123), it follows that three types of aspect are jointly expressed on the same verb, i.e., inchoative (phasal), imperfective (perfectivity), and activity (inherent). It is partly on the basis of this type of multiple aspectual expressions that the aspectual system in Obolo is categorized as having three components, i.e., inherent, perfectivity, and phasal aspects.

In (123), the inchoative is marked by the morpheme *ní*, the imperfective by *kí*, while the verb itself expresses an activity. While activity is lexical and is expressed by the nature of the verb, both the inchoative and the imperfective are morphologically marked. All three of them occur on the same verb root *kọ́t* 'sing'.

(123) í-yâ-yàkà   í-ní-kí-kọ́t
   3SG-REDUP-turn^(ITER) NSP-INC-IMPF-sing^(ACT)
   He continued to sing again.

Beyond co-occurrence, the restrictions imposed by each aspect type on the interpretation of the other are discussed in this section in the order of (1) perfectivity and inherent aspects, (2) phasal aspects and perfectivity, and (3) phasal and inherent aspects.

5.4.1 Perfectivity and inherent aspects

Both perfective and imperfective co-occur with all the subtypes of the inherent aspect. Each of these co-occurrences is discussed separately in this section, starting with those involving the perfective aspect.

Perfective and states. When the perfective co-occurs with states, it does not include any end point since states are atelic. The view of perfectivity adopted in Obolo is that a situation is viewed from the outside and seen as a whole, without regard to the internal constituency of the situation. Therefore, states can be perfective. A perfective stative situation is exemplified in (124). The perfective is unmarked in Obolo, and state, an inherent aspect, is lexical, thus carrying no morphological marking. Therefore, nothing is marked in the example.

(124) ífè chà   árâñ ó-kúp mé ísí
      people DDEM^pl oil 3sg-stay PREP front
      There was oil in front of those people.

Perfective and activities and semelfactives. When the perfective occurs with atelic activities and semelfactives, it presents the event as a whole, implying some sort of arbitrary end point, since activities and semelfactives are both dynamic. The co-occurrence of the perfective with activities and semelfactives is illustrated in (125) and (126), respectively. In (125) there is no indication that the dogs were caught or when they were caught, or that the chase was terminated, or when it was terminated. But the event is presented in the discourse as a whole event that did happen. This discourse context implies an apparent termination point, which at best is arbitrary.

(125) mî-ĺi-lábá   íbó í-kàná   érè   mé ìyâkwùt
      cpl-REDUP-chase dog NSP-round   place PREP yesterday
      They chased dogs around the place yesterday.

The same argument applies in (126). The child coughing is packaged and presented as a whole, as an event that did take place. Since it is not presented as something that was happening at the moment of speech, an end point, an arbitrary end point, is assumed.

(126) gwúñ í-kọ̀lọ́   úkộm
      child NSP-cough cough
      The child coughed.

Perfective and accomplishments and achievements. Since accomplishments and achievements are telic and have inherent perfectivity, co-occurrence with the perfective poses no problems. These co-occurrences are illustrated in (127) and (128). In the two examples, though the situations are presented as wholes, each has a natural end point built into it.

(127) èmâ mî-tèt   ówùwà íŕîñ
      3pl cpl-catch   many fish
      They caught a lot of fish.

(128) ènyì í-sǐ-ré   ókwááñ
      2pl cpl-CNS-reach   big^river
      when you (pl) reach the big river

Imperfective. The imperfective co-occurs with all types of the inherent aspect: states, activities, semelfactives, accomplishments, and

Aspect

achievements. Since activities and accomplishments both have durative internal structure which is compatible with the imperfective, they are not discussed in this section. The section will concentrate on those associations that do not seem to be compatible. These include: progressive and states, progressive and achievements, imperfective and semelfactives, and nonprogressive imperfective and states.

Progressive and states. Much is said in the literature concerning the co-occurrence of the progressive with states. The progressive implies a processual meaning which in turn implies change of state and phasality. States are nonphasal, i.e., do not have internal temporal structure, and so cannot be presented as ongoing or in-progress. However, speakers do choose to use states in the progressive, e.g., the English progressive stative *she is being quiet*.

In Obolo, the association of the progressive with states has two possible interpretations. The first is continuity in the given state. This is illustrated in (129) where the speaker asks whether the hearer is still continuing to remain in the state of being brilliant at school.

(129) ì-rè   òwù   ò-gá-!kí-ri̯ọ́ọ́ñ   íkpá   sí
3sg-be 2sg 2sg-PLOC-IMPF-know book still
Are you still brilliant (at school)?

The second possible interpretation is that, in such an association, the progressive seems to change the stative situation into a somewhat dynamic phasal situation. This situation is best described as "gradual-becoming" or "becoming-more-and-more." It is exemplified in (130), which is best interpreted as 'you are getting to know me more and more'.

(130) òwù   ò-gá-!kí-ri̯ọ́ọ́ñ   èmì
2sg 2sg-PLOC-IMPF-know 1sg
You are knowing me.

Progressive and achievements. When the progressive co-occurs with an achievement (punctual, telic) verb, it has the effect of transforming it into an accomplishment (durative, telic) with a schema that contains a durative phase before the end point. This is illustrated in (131). In this example, the state of the victim gradually becomes worse and worse until eventual death. Literally, the example says that death is progressively catching up with the victim, that is, one by one the vital parts of the body are becoming lifeless. At this point, it can still be said of the victim that s/he is not completely dead (lit. s/he has not finished dying). This is one of the most effective means of distinguishing between accomplishments and achievements. While this statement can be made for accomplishments, it cannot be made for achievements.

(131) ò-kí-kwú
 3sg-IMPF-die
 S/he is dying.

The progressive focuses on the internal structure of the accomplishment. But since achievements are punctual, the focus of the progressive rather adds a durative phase that leads up to the end point, thus effectively transforming the achievement into an accomplishment.

Imperfective and semelfactives. The imperfective gives an iterative interpretation with semelfactives. Since semelfactives are punctual, they have no internal temporal structure. They have no phase leading up to the event, and no phase leading away from it, so the effect of the imperfective on it is to reiterate the event. This is illustrated in (132).

(132) ò-kí-kòló úkọ̀m
 3sg-IMPF-cough cough
 S/he is coughing (repeatedly).

Nonprogressive imperfective and states. In the same way, when the nonprogressive imperfective, such as continuous or habitual, co-occurs with statives, it gives an interpretation of habitual iterativity. This is illustrated in (133) which is a resultative construction preceded by a conditional clause. The result is also generic, indicated by the generic marker ràbí, which makes it something that happened more than once. The imperfective marking makes the resulting state something that always happened whenever the condition was met. In this way the state is reiterated habitually.

(133) àkpà î-ràbí í-kí-tóp
 corn 3sg-GEN NSP-IMPF-delicious
 (And) maize would (always) be delicious.

5.4.2 Perfectivity and phasal aspects

As already illustrated in example (123), the perfective co-occurs with all types of phasal aspects without any change in meaning. But the imperfective has the effect of stretching inceptives and completives out into multi-phased subphases. This is the same effect as the progressive has on achievements.

5.5 Phasal and inherent aspects

To a large extent, co-occurrence of phasal aspect with inherent aspect depends on two parameters: process and the phase of focus of the phasal aspect. Processual aspects on both sides are easily compatible. Phasal aspects such as inceptives, completives, and duratives which imply a process (they are phases in a process) may co-occur easily with inherent aspects such as activities and, to a large extent, accomplishments, which also have a process in their schema. Phasal aspects such as inchoatives and immediative, which focus on the boundary between two consecutive situations, seem to be able to co-occur with many inherent aspects with no change in meaning. Beyond these, co-occurrence results in other meanings.

Inceptive, completive, and durative with activities and accomplishments. Inceptives, completives, and duratives co-occur with activities without changing the meaning of activities, as illustrated in (134)–(136), respectively, where they simply add their own phasal aspectual meaning to the inherent aspectual sense of the activities.

(134) î-bènè   í-kọ̀t   ókwà
 3sg-begin NSP-sing song
 S/he started to sing a song.

(135) î-kọ̀t   ókwà í-sáñá
 3sg-sing song NSP-finish
 S/he finished singing a song.

(136) î-kọ̀t   ókwà í-kọ́t   í-kọ́t   í-kọ́t
 3sg-sing song NSP-sing NSP-sing NSP-sing
 S/he sang a song for a long time.

With accomplishments, only the inceptive and completive can co-occur without altering the meaning of accomplishments. This is illustrated in (137) and (138), respectively. The reason is that since accomplishments are telic, and the focus is on the end result, they have natural end points, and they imply a process that has a definite beginning and a definite end.

(137) î-bènè   í-bọ́p   úwù
 3sg-begin NSP-build house
 S/he started to build a house.

(138) î-bòp   úwù   í-sáñà
      3sg-build house NSP-finish
      S/he finished building a house.

Without any modification, the durative cannot co-occur with accomplishments without implying an additional meaning. The reason is that the focus of the accomplishment is on the end result, and the process between the beginning of the accomplishment and its end cannot be extended beyond what is necessary. Therefore, example (139) has two meanings. The first is the usual combination of the meaning of the phasal aspect, durative, with that of the accomplishment. The second implies many objects, that is, in this case, more than one house. This indeterminacy of meaning would not occur in English which always requires number marking on the object.

(139) î-bòp   úwù   í-bóp   í-bóp   í-bóp
      3sg-build house NSP-build   NSP-build   NSP-build
      S/he built a house for a long time *or* (s/he built many houses).

To avoid the second meaning, the object, would need to be modified, e.g., by means of a definite article, as illustrated in (140).

(140) î-bòp   úwù   yà   í-bóp   í-bóp   í-bóp
      3sg-build house DDEM^sg   NSP-build   NSP-build   NSP-build
      S/he built the house for a long time.

Inceptive, completive, and durative with states, semelfactives, and achievements. The inceptive, completive, and durative seem to have the same effects on semelfactives and achievements. Like the progressive already discussed, when the inceptive, completive, and durative co-occur with semelfactives, they give an iterative meaning since the semelfactive only has a single phase, and this group of phasal aspects are processual, as illustrated in (140)–(143), respectively.

(141) gwùñ   î-bènè   í-kòló   úkôm
      child NSP-begin   NSP-cough   cough
      The child started to cough. (implying, 'then s/he coughed many times')

(142) gwúñ   î-kòló   úkôm   í-sáñá
      child 3sg-cough   cough   NSP-finish
      The child finished coughing. (implying 's/he finished the series of coughing')

(143) gwúñ î-kòló   úkộm í-kòló   í-kòló   í-kòló
      child 3sg-cough cough NSP-cough NSP-cough NSP-cough
      The child coughed and coughed and coughed.

Like the progressive, which is also processual, the inceptive and completive have the effect of transforming achievements into accomplishments. The reason, as given above for the progressive, is that the achievement is single-phased, and this single phase by itself constitutes a change of state. The effect of these processual phasal aspects is to create a phase before the single state-changing phase in the achievement, thus transforming the achievement effectively into an accomplishment. For certain achievement verbs, a second meaning, multiplicity of objects, may be added. The inceptive with achievement is illustrated in (144) and the completive with achievement in (145). The (a) examples only change achievements into accomplishments, while the (b) examples, in addition to that, also include an interpretation of plural objects.

(144) a. úrá î-bènè   í-chép
         sun 3sg-begin NSP-lost
         The sun began to set.

      b. î-bènè   í-múñ   òfùt
         3sg-begin NSP-see bird
         S/he started spotting birds.

(145) a. úrá î-chèp   í-sáñá
         sun 3sg-lost NSP-finish
         The sun finished setting (i.e., the sun has set completely).

      b. î-mùñ   òfùt í-sáñá
         3sg-spot bird NSP-finish
         S/he finished spotting birds.

On the other hand, when the durative co-occurs with accomplishments, the result is an iterative meaning, the same effect that the progressive has with semelfactives. Therefore, both parts of example (146) have iterative meaning. In (146b), there is also the added meaning of multiplicity of objects. This meaning is not possible in (a) because of the singularity of the sun. Therefore, (a) may be referring to many days of sunset, rather than a single day with many sunsets.

(146) a. úrá î-chép   í-chép   í-chép   í-chép
         sun 3sg-lost NSP-lost NSP-lost NSP-lost
         The sun set many times.

b. î-mùñ   òfùt   í-múñ   í-múñ   í-múñ
   3sg-see bird NSP-see NSP-see NSP-see
   S/he spotted birds several times.

There is no such uniformity of results, as discussed above, when the inceptive, completive, and durative co-occur with states. When the inceptive co-occurs with states, the result is an inchoative meaning of 'becoming', i.e., a state comes into being, as shown in (147). When the completive and the durative are used with states, as in (148)–(149), respectively, they encode a superlative degree of the state which is actually an idiomatic expression in the language. Each of these meanings are reflected in the English gloss.

(147) úwù   î-bènè   í-jààñ
       house NSP-begin   NSP-beautiful
       The house has become (or started to become) beautiful.

(148) úwù   î-jààñ   í-sáñá
       house 3sg-beautiful   NSP-finish
       The house is completely beautiful (it can't be better).

(149) úwù   î-jààñ   í-jààñ   í-jààñ   í-jààñ
       house 3sg-beautiful NSP-beautiful NSP-beautiful NSP-beautiful
       The house is very very beautiful.

Iteratives with inherent aspects. The iterative generally implies break(s) or pause(es) and resumption(s) of the same situation. So it easily co-occurs with activities and semelfactives without any change of meaning. When the iterative co-occurs with states, accomplishments, and achievements, other meanings result, as illustrated in (150)–(152), respectively. With states, the iterative implies a break followed by a resumption in the state of affairs. With accomplishments and achievements, it may imply multiple objects, since they involve situations that usually cannot be reversed.

(150) m̀bọ́m   î-kpọ̀k   í-nwọ́n
       fishing   3sg-ITER   NSP-good
       Fishing is good again (implying 'it was once good, then bad, then good again now').

(151) ògwù   ńjìn î-kpọ̀k   í-tét   ìrîñ
       DET^sg   net   3sg-ITER NSP-catch   fish
       The net-fisherman has caught fish again (implying 'he caught fish before, and now has caught another one').

(152) gògó î-kpọ̀k í-bùm úmọ̀ọ́ñ
Gogo 3sg-ITER NSP-break mirror
Gogo has broken a mirror again (implying 'he broke one before, and has now broken another').

Immediative and inchoative with inherent aspects. Since immediative focuses on the boundary between two consecutive situations, it implies the end point of one situation and the beginning point of another. Although activities have no natural end points, when immediative occurs between two activities, or an activity followed by another inherent aspect, it implies an end point, albeit an arbitrary end point, of the first activity. Therefore, immediative can co-occur with all phasal inherent aspects without any change in meaning. But when it occurs with states, which are nonphasal, it results in the inchoative meaning of 'becoming', as illustrated in (153). The verb marked for immediative is bolded.

(153) *í-jâ-jààñ*　　ólóm　ó-bê-bènè　í-kí-nú　mé
3sg-REDUP-beautiful husband 3sg-REDUP-begin NSP-IMPF-come PREP

lék
body
As soon as she became beautiful suitors began to come (to seek) to marry her.

Like immediative, the inchoative, which also focuses on the boundary between two consecutive situations, co-occurs with all phasal inherent aspects without any change in meaning. The inchoative generally implies that a state of affairs which was not present before has come into being. With states, it assumes the meaning 'becoming' as illustrated in (154).

(154) *í-bâ-bàlà*　　lék　mè　*í-ní-jááñ*　ènénén
3sg-REDUP-decorate body CONJ NSP-INC-beautiful very^much
She decorated herself and became very beautiful.

5.6 Aspect and tense

The correlation between present tense and imperfective aspect, which is commonly held a priori in the literature does not reveal much about these categories in Obolo, because the imperfective (the marked member of the perfective/imperfective opposition) co-occurs with both future tense (marked) and nonfuture (unmarked) time references. On the contrary, the imperfective is even found to co-occur many more times with past than with present time reference in two sample texts (PROGS and WB) in my database as illustrated in (155).

(155) Imperfective with different time references

Text	Present	Past	Other	Total
PROGS	12	18	4	34
WB	0	25	13	38
Total	12 (17%)	43 (60%)	17 (23%)	72

In (155), the present and past time references are distinguished by means of temporal adverbials. The category "other" consists of occurrences of *ki* in quoted speeches and in tense-neutral generic expressions. As the figures in (155) show, out of the 72 occurrences of the imperfective in both PROGS and WB texts, only 12 (17%) co-occur with present-time reference, while 43 (60%) co-occur with past-time reference. This means that events may be presented as ongoing in all time references, more in fact in past time than in the present, even in a comparative (past versus present) text like PROGS.

On the other hand, the correlation between past-time reference and perfective aspect is revealing in Obolo. The perfective aspect implies completion or termination; therefore, it tends to correlate with the past-time reference especially because the past tense carries no morphological marking. This fact is borne out in the same two sample texts in my database as illustrated in (156). In this table, out of the 266 occurrences of the perfective in both texts, 158 (59%) are in past-time reference, while only 24 (9%) are in present-time reference.

(156) Perfective with different time referenses

Text	Present	Past	Future	Other	Total
PROGS	24	41	6	41	112
WB	0	117	2	35	154
Total	24 (9%)	158 (59%)	8 (3%)	76 (29%)	266 (100%)

The combined figures in (155)–(156) show that of the 36 occurrences of the present-time reference in both texts, only 12 (33%) are in the imperfective, while 24 (67%) are in the perfective. Also out of the 201 occurrences of the past-time reference in both texts, only 43 (21%) are in the imperfective, while 158 (79%) are in the perfective. This implies a weak correlation between the imperfective and the present-time reference, and a strong correlation between the perfective and past-time reference.

Apart from showing a stronger tendency for the perfective to correlate with past time reference than for the imperfective to correlate with present-time reference, both tables also jointly illustrate the fact that both the perfective and the imperfective do co-occur freely with all time references: present, past, future, and even with the tense-neutral generic. Examples (157) and (158) illustrate co-occurrences of the imperfective with past-time reference, and perfective with the future-tense, respectively.

(157) èbí ǹté-ǹté kìjì kpè-kí-má
DET^pl father-father 1pl^POSS cpl^NEG-IMPF-like
our fore-fathers did not use to like

(158) mè òwù kpǫ̀ mè mô-gbè ǫ́mǫ̂
CONJ 2sg 2sg^IMP-look CONJ 3sg^FUT-suit 3sg
and you (sg) look (and see) whether it will suit him

In the same way, inherent and phasal aspects also co-occur with the different time references. Examples (157) and (158) illustrate the co-occurrence of states with past time and future tense. The iterative maintains its meaning in all tenses, but the co-occurrence of the inchoative with the future tense sometimes gives an immediate future meaning, as illustrated in (159). However, when accompanied by the adverb *săbùm* 'before', the inchoative does not give the immediate future meaning (see chapter 3).

(159) mô-nǐ-sí éwé
3sg^FUT-INC-go market
s/he is about to go to market

In summary, all aspects (perfectivity, inherent, and phasal aspects) co-occur with all time references without change of meaning, except the inchoative which gives an immediate future meaning when it co-occurs with the future tense, without the adverb *săbùm* 'before'. Somewhat exhaustive lists of co-occurrence of tense, aspect, and the perfect with mood and focus are given in the appendix.

6
An Overview of Tense and Aspect in Discourse

This chapter reviews some of the literature with regard to the domain of tense and aspect in general and concludes that it is not a matter of either the sentence or discourse, but a combination of both. The choice of a particular tense or aspect is motivated by the discourse and also dependent on the inherent sentential semantic properties of the particular concerned tense or aspect. The discussion of tense and aspect in the sentence correlates with the referential component of Halliday and Hassan (1976) while the discussion of the functions of tense and aspect in discourse structure correlates with their textual component. Tense and aspect are among the resources available for organizing a discourse in terms of coherence and grounding.

Since the role of tense and aspect in the structure of discourse is most clearly visible in grounding, the foreground-background distinction (see §6.1), out of the many properties of discourse structure, is the focus of this research. First, however, some general and fundamental issues are discussed in the rest of this chapter as a background against which the rest of the study is to be understood. These include: issues concerning tense and aspect in relation to discourse, i.e., the domain of tense and aspect; monologue discourse; foreground and background in narratives; and grounding in discourse in general.

6.1 Domain of tense and aspect

Opinions are divided in the literature about where tense and aspect categories really belong, whether they are a sentential property or a discourse property, that is, whether their meanings are explainable exclusively in terms of their semantic functions in the sentence or in terms of their discourse functions.

Smith (1983:480) takes aspect to be a property of the sentence, the relation between aspect and discourse is via the contribution of the meaning of the sentence to the meaning of the text or discourse. This indirect relationship presents discourse as a passive receiver of aspectual meaning. In Truth Conditional Semantics (Lewis 1972),[33] truth conditions alone are the key to meaning. That is, it is the meaning of a sentence that determines the conditions under which the sentence would be true. Another viewpoint, Kamp (1985), says that meaning is what receivers grasp when they understand a sentence. He explains this using formal representations that formulate mental models of understanding. However, neither Kamp nor Lewis uses natural spontaneous texts to illustrate their theory.

Recent works in discourse analysis have argued that aspects derive their primary meaning from their discourse function.[34] These works describe the relation between aspect and discourse in a manner exactly opposite to Smith and the others mentioned in the paragraph above. They argue that it is discourse that motivates the choice and use of aspects. In other words, while the first group argues that aspect is a property of the sentence, the second group argues that aspect is rather a property of the discourse.

Actually, these two views are not as conflicting as they seem to be. I see them as complementary. I think that the choice of an aspect is motivated by discourse, based on inherent semantic properties of the aspect. Ehrlich (1987) takes this point of view in her discussion of the meaning of the English past progressive and argues that the global discourse functions of foreground and background do not adequately account for aspectual alternations in texts. She points out that both sentential semantic properties and the local discourse context of an aspect are crucial to the interpretation of the aspect.

By the statement that the distribution of tense and aspect cannot be properly accounted for without mention of the distinction between main line and supportive material, Longacre (1983) places the locus of tense

---

[33]See Lewis 1972, Comrie (1976), and Lyons (1997), who also present aspect as a sentential property.

[34]Hopper 1979b, 1982a and b; Li, Thompson, and Thompson 1979; Dry 1981; Chvany 1985; and Thelin 1990b.

and aspect in discourse structure in foreground/background distinction. The bond between tense and aspect and grounding in discourse is also indicated by Jones and Jones (1984) in their work on Mesoamerican languages, who say that light can best be shed on the function of aspect/tense/mood morphemes in connected discourse in these languages through the concepts of foregrounded and backgrounded information. Another work that has related tense and aspect to discourse grounding is Schram (1979). In his analysis of different types of discourse in Mazatec, Schram found that the distinguishing tense/aspect marking of the foreground is what he calls distant past complete for narrative, generic, or customary tense for explanatory discourse, and future incomplete for hortatory. Each discourse type has what he calls a global tense,[35] i.e., an overarching temporal frame within which the temporal structures in the discourse are interpreted.

6.2 Monologue discourse

Since the texts on which this study is based are all various types of monologues, i.e., narrative, procedural, compare-and-contrast, expository, and hortatory monologues, it is useful to consider some of the studies that have already been made on monologues.

According to Longacre (1983), the term discourse covers two areas of linguistic concern, namely, the analysis of dialogue, and the analysis of monologue. By dialogue he means an interactive discourse that involves more than one interlocutor, with all the interlocutors participating actively. By monologue he means a discourse delivered by one person.

According to him, one initial concern in analyzing monologue discourse is discourse typology. The characteristics of individual discourses, can be neither described, predicted, nor analyzed without resort to a classification of discourse types. All monologue discourses are not the same. For instance, there are differences among fairy tales, novels, short stories, first person accounts, newspaper reports of events, essays, scientific papers, sermons, pep talks, political speeches, recipes, do-it-yourself books, etc. However, there are similarities between some of these types. Fairy tales and short stories are both types of stories; essays and scientific papers share much in common; some commonalities also exist between sermons and pep talks, and between recipes and do-it-yourself books.

Longacre proposes four different parameters for distinguishing among discourse types. These are contingent temporal succession, agent orientation, projection, and tension. Contingent temporal succession refers to a framework of temporal succession in which an event is contingent on

---

[35] In Schram's system (1979), "tense" includes both tense and aspect.

previous event(s). Agent orientation refers to orientation towards agents with at least a partial identity of agent reference running through the discourse. Projection has to do with a situation or action which is contemplated, enjoined, or anticipated but not realized. The fourth, tension, has to do with whether a discourse reflects a struggle or polarization of some sort. According to him, the first two, contingent temporal succession and agent orientation are broad parameters because they only make broad-based distinctions, while the last two, projection and tension, are narrow parameters because they help to make fine distinctions between related discourse types.

Longacre's fourth parameter tension helps to distinguish between compare-and-contrast and the ordinary expository texts in my database, both of which belong in the expository genre. While compare-and-contrast is plus tension because of polarization in the contrast, the latter is minus tension because it does not involve polarization.

6.3 Foreground and background in narrative discourse[36]

According to Dry (1992:438) several concepts masquerade under the single term foreground, the reason being that foreground is of interest to many disciplines, and each group defines it based on the nature of the texts studied in that discipline. Among these groups are literary critics, psycholinguists, and discourse analysts.

Dry (1992) and Fleischman (1985) list the defining properties of narrative prominence normally associated with foreground in the scholarly literature. However, Dry (1992:438) finds two major concepts implicit in the definitions: importance and salience, each with subdefinitions.[37] Importance is defined in terms of thematicity, human arguments or intrinsic human properties (e.g., volitionality), causality, and in terms of form or arrangement of the events (sometimes called definitional importance). Formal importance may be seen in the iconic arrangement of the events in the order in which they occurred in the real world. It may also be seen in temporal succession. These set apart events on the narrative timeline/eventline from other events. Salience is defined in terms of unexpectedness, figural properties (i.e., smallness, closure, detachment,

---

[36] For full discussions of foreground and background and other issues concerning this distinction, see Labov and Waletzky (1967); Labov (1972); Grimes (1975); Hopper (1979b); Hopper and Thompson (1980); Wallace (1982); Fleischman (1985); van Peer (1986); Thompson (1987); Givón (1987); and Dry (1981, 1992). This subsection is based on Dry's work (1992), *Foregrounding: An Assessment.*

[37] See Dry (1992:439ff) for the descriptions, explanations, and sources of each of the subdefinitions.

An Overview of Tense and Aspect in Discourse

dimensionality, etc.), and cognitive accessibility. Dry illustrates these definitions in the figure reproduced in (160).

By this figure Dry refutes a crucial assumption that importance and salience coincide, which is commonly held a priori in the literature. According to Dry, importance and salience do not necessarily coincide. The lack of coincidence is shown in the fact that the properties associated with salience do not ensure centrality or importance. For instance cognitive accessibility may obtain of any recently mentioned items whether significant or insignificant. Also, unexpectedness and figural properties may characterize important as well as unimportant textual elements.

(160) Definitions of the foreground (Dry 1992:438)

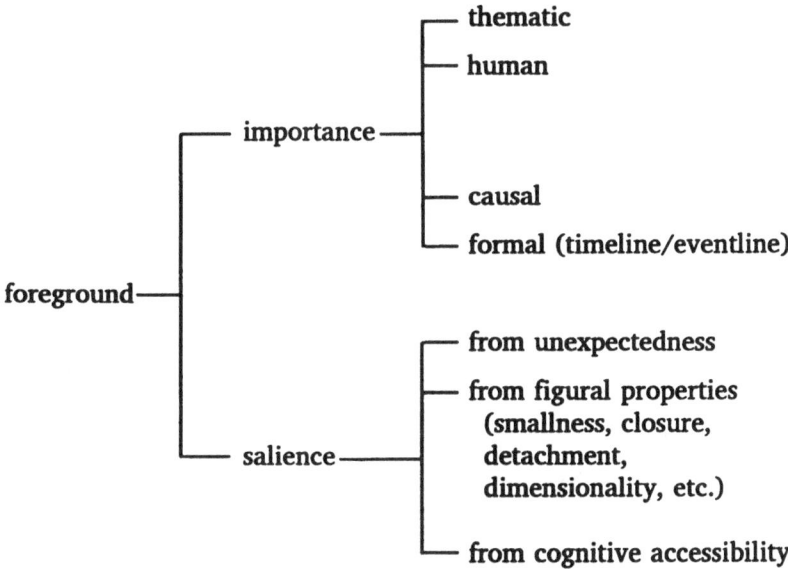

Dry (1992:441ff.) points out some assumptions that are not represented in the figure. The first is that it does not adequately reflect the conceptual diversity involved in foregrounding. For instance, among other things, it does not adequately represent the cluster concept approach to foreground, commonly manifested as a collection of properties, not all of which need to be present to identify a passage as foreground. Secondly, she points out that the figure does not portray the many overlaps among the categories, e.g., coincidence of highly transitive and temporally successive clauses.

The final assumptions not represented by the figure are the controversies currently linked to these definitions. Dry points out and addresses some of these controversies, which include: (1) whether or not foreground is equivalent to temporally successive clauses, (2) whether the foreground/background distinction is best perceived as binary or continuum-like, (3) whether foreground is a relative or absolute determination, and (4) whether the application of the visual theory of figure and ground to textual foregrounding has more than metaphoric import.

Regarding whether or not foreground is equivalent to temporally successive clauses, Dry (p. 442) argues that temporally successive clauses have a definitional importance in that they constitute a necessary, perhaps sufficient, identificational condition for a narrative, and are often highly transitive. She also points out that although unelaborated temporally successive clauses usually convey the central point of the story, temporal succession does not have thematic importance over other narrative phenomena.

For the issue of whether the foreground/background distinction is best seen as binary or continuum-like, Dry appeals to the cluster-concept feature of the foreground. She points out that "where a language has more than one way of marking foreground, different combinations of markers allow for varying degrees of foreground. This is what gives the cluster-concept approach to foreground its scalar character" (1992:446).

As to whether foreground is absolute or relative, Dry (p. 445) argues that foreground may be relative in literary texts because it is linked to "point of view" and, in this way, is contextually determined, that is, events are filtered through some conciousness which may promote some situations to importance and demote others. However, foreground tends to be presented more as an absolute concept in discussions on discourse analysis in which overt marking or some stable identification of the foreground, e.g., by special verb forms, is emphasized.

Regarding the application of the visual figure/ground theory to textual foregrounding, Dry argues that this application cannot have more than metaphorical import since there is no one-to-one correlation between the visual characteristics proposed in Wallace (1982) and their corresponding textual analogues.

6.4 Grounding in discourse in general

The majority of scholars who have written on foreground and background in discourse have written almost exclusively on narrative.

Some of these scholars, however, have hinted that grounding is universal to all discourse regardless of type. Wallace (1982) points out that the foreground/background distinction is universal to all discourse genres, and that the foreground includes the more important events of a narrative, the more important steps of a procedure, the central points of an exposition, and the main characters or entities involved in an episode, while the background includes events of lesser importance, subsidiary procedures, secondary points, descriptions, elaborations, digressions, and minor characters or things.

These general definitions suggest the universality of the distinction between foreground and background. As Longacre puts it, "The different sorts of texts have differing main lines of development: Narrative text has a story line; procedural text has a line of procedure; hortatory/persuasive text has a line of exhortation...; and expository text has a line of exposition" (1989b:415). Other scholars support the view that all discourse has some sort of "main line," including monologue discourse types. The fact that the main line of one discourse type is different from that of another discourse type is supported by the texts in my database, which are all monologues. In each of the texts, there are main lines and embellishments, but the components of each of these differ according to discourse type. With respect to tense and aspect, the main lines in these texts exhibit different characteristics. This is the topic of the remaining chapters of this study.

The following quotation gives the best general definition of foreground and background in discourse without reference to any particular discourse type. The linguistic features that mark these types differ, depending on the speaker's communicative goals. Therein lies the basis for differences in discourse types.

> Users of a language are constantly required to design their utterances in accord with their own communicative goals and with their perception of their listeners' needs. Yet, in any speaking situation, some parts of what is said are more relevant than others. That part of a discourse which does not immediately and crucially contribute to the speaker's goal, but which merely assists, amplifies, or comments on it, is referred to as background. By contrast, the material which supplies the main points of the discourse is known as foreground. (Hopper and Thompson 1980:280)

The linguistic features that mark the foreground and background of the narrative discourse have been thoroughly described. But in dealing with grounding in other discourse types, one is very much in an uncharted territory. However, works of Longacre and his associates,[38] and especially, in my area of interest, the works of McArthur (1979) on Aguacatec,[39] and Schram (1979) on Mazatec of Jalapa de Diaz[40] provide

---

[38]See especially Longacre's works on Philippine (1968) and Papua New Guinea (1972) languages for a more comprehensive discussion.

[39]Aguacatec is a Mesoamerican language spoken in Aguacatán municipality in the southeastern part of the department of Huehuetenango in Guatemala (McArthur 1979).

[40]Mazatec of Jalapa de Diaz is a Popolucan language of the Otomanguean family spoken by about 8,000 people in the district of Tuxtepec, Oaxaca, Mexico (Schram 1979).

a good base from which to start. In terms of the linguistic features that mark grounding in nonnarrative discourse types, these two articles present the first systematic analysis of their kind with respect to tense and aspect.

However, certain features of the narrative foreground are seen to apply to nonnarrative foreground as well. The most significant of these is the cluster concept of the foreground. Apart from tense and aspect, mood and modality also play a crucial part in the foreground of nonnarrative genres. Longacre (1968) has also shown that the overall structure, as well as connectives between sentences and paragraphs, serves to distinguish between discourse types and thus the notion of a cluster concept of the foreground holds across discourse types. Since the focus of this study is only on tense and aspect and not on any other feature of grounding, I concentrate on these and mention other features only when necessary.

Reichman (1985) and Dahlgren (1988) relate the structure of a discourse genre to the set of interclausal relations that exist in the genre, saying that narrative, argument, news article, conversation, and scientific report each have their own content structure, that is, their own set of relations between clauses. This is not to say that each and every discourse type has a unique set of relations. Since a particular relation may occur in more than one discourse type, what this statement means is that each discourse genre has a set of relations that are dominant in it.

To isolate the foreground and background in any text without regard to its discourse type, I rely on the relational structure models proposed by Mann and Thompson (1987) and Callow and Callow (1992). Both of these models have the capacity to isolate nuclear and supportive materials in any text regardless of discourse types. Texts are broken down into pairs of spans, which in my case are simple clauses consisting of a single verb (or a serial verb construction) each. When adjacent clauses are compared, in relation with one another, some may be nuclear and the other(s) may be supportive material, referred to as satellites. In these two models, as the same relations apply from the low levels, e.g., between clauses, to the high levels, e.g., between paragraphs, the notion of nucleus and satellite also applies at the various levels. A string of the major nuclei in the text give the main-line information of the text regardless of the discourse classification of the text. By the same token, the satellites together form the background information of the text. Nuclei may exist without satellites, but satellites cannot exist without nuclei.

6.5 Methodology and terminology

The methodology followed in this section of the study is as follows. First, the texts are split up into clauses, then the clauses are coded for types, i.e., main, coordinate, paratactic, subordinate, complement, and embedded clauses, and for temporal structures, i.e., tenses and aspects of all types. Secondly, the clauses are charted using one of the two text structure relational models developed by Mann and Thompson (1987) or Callow and Callow (1992). From the charts two important components of discourse coherence are observed: (1) the organization of the text in terms of the introduction, main body, and the conclusion, as well as the arrangement of paragraphs within each of these sections; and (2) the relations between clauses and between paragraphs. These relations distinguish between nuclear and supportive material. Thirdly, the paragraphs in all the sections are discussed in terms of the general distribution of tense and aspect where they are sometimes used differently from one section to another depending on discourse type. This discussion comes under the heading of structure. Fourthly, grounding in the particular discourse type is discussed based on the nuclear versus nonnuclear material identified from the chart. Fifthly, the distribution of tense and aspect in the identified foreground and background material is discussed. To avoid confusion, note that throughout the discussion, aspectual labels all refer to aspects, not to verb meanings. These are labels such as perfective, continuous, and habitual for perfectivity; state/stative, activity, accomplishment, achievement, and semelfactive for inherent aspect; and inceptive/ingressive, completive, durative, iterative, immediative, and inchoative for phasal aspect.

As mentioned earlier, the texts studied in this research are narrative, procedural, expository, compare-and-contrast, and hortatory monologues. The compare-and-contrast text is a type of expository discourse, but it is different enough, in terms of tense and aspect, to warrant a separate discussion on its own in chapter 11.

I use the terms foreground and background for mainline and supportive information, respectively, in all discourse types. This means that the characterization of foreground and background is different from one discourse type to another, depending on the linguistic features that constitute it in a given discourse type. For instance, the foreground of a narrative discourse may be characterized as consisting of, among other features, transitive, temporally ordered clauses with perfective verbs, usually in past tense, indicative mood, etc., while the foreground of another discourse genre may be defined differently.

Another term that is widely used in the chapters that follow is paragraph. One factor in common in all definitions of paragraph is that they are based on both content and surface marking. Since the emphasis of this study is not on the structure of the paragraph, the term paragraph is used here to mean a set of clauses that describe the same topic or subtopic and may be marked syntactically as a unit separate from the adjacent units that have similar structures. For instance, in the procedural discourse, the paragraph would consist of the consequential or conditional clause(s) with all the other clauses that follow, i.e., a combination of the protasis and the apodosis. Each of these structures contains one topic or many related subtopics, and is marked morphosyntactically as a separate unit.

In referring to types of clauses, main clause refers to an independent clause that is neither coordinate nor paratactic. A coordinate clause refers to a clause that is conjoined to the main clause by an overt conjunction, while a paratactic clause refers to an independent clause that is simply juxtaposed with the main clause but not conjoined by an overt conjunction. A subordinate clause refers to any of two groups of dependent clauses, namely hypotactic (usually adverbial clause) in one group, and embedded clause, a cover term for complement clauses and relative clauses, in the second group.

7
Tense and Aspect in Narrative Discourse

In every way, narrative discourse is the most studied of all the four widely accepted discourse genres (narrative, expository, procedural, and hortatory), and much of what is written about it has already been discussed in chapter 6. However, a few pertinent facts still need to be mentioned as a backdrop for the discussion that follows in this chapter. According to Fleischman (1991), (1) narratives refer to specific experiences that occurred in some past world (real or imagined) and are accordingly reported in tenses of the past; (2) while narratives contain both sequentially ordered events and nonsequential collateral material (description, commentary), it is the sequentially ordered events that constitute the backbone of a narration; and (3) the order of narrative units in the text parallels the order of events in the world modelled by the text.

In a narrative sequence, the completion of one event is implied by the inception of the following event, a fact which gives rise to the correlation between the perfective aspect and the past tense. The property of completion, which is inherent in the perfective aspect, explains why perfective verbs, in narratives, imply sequentiality.

7.1 Tense and aspect in narrative foreground and background

The past tense is the dominant tense in narratives, and Hopper (1979b) proposes a correlation between the perfective aspect and narrative foreground.[41] Dry (1981) concludes that change of state, not perfectivity, is the crucial factor in narrative time shift. These two views of aspects in the foreground actually complement, rather than contrast with, each other.

Both Hopper and Dry emphasize the contribution of two types of aspect to the narrative foreground. While Hopper emphasizes the contribution of perfectivity aspect, Dry, on the other hand, emphasizes the contribution of inherent aspect to the narrative foreground with change of state as a property of inherent aspect. This property distinguishes between states and nonstates in the inherent aspect. States do not involve any change of state, but all nonstates do. Therefore, Dry's proposal is that nonstativity is the crucial factor in the narrative time shift. Since states do not involve change of states, they cannot shift the narrative time.

The imperfective nonstatives cannot shift narrative time, because even though they involve change of states, they are not perfective. Therefore, it is not just change of state that advances narrative time. On the other hand, as the imperfective nonstatives cannot shift narrative time, neither can perfective states, because, even though perfective states are perfective, they do not involve any change of states. Therefore, it is neither perfectivity by itself nor nonstativity by itself that shifts narrative time, but rather a combination of both perfectivity and nonstativity. Furthermore, the phasal aspects also contribute to narrative grounding.

Longacre (1989) arranges narrative foreground/background material in bands on a continuum, which he refers to as a universal verb ranking schema,[42] in order of salience, from most to least salient. His verb ranking band for English, which shows how the English tense and aspect categories function in narrative structure, is given in (161).

According to him, the bands may be different from one language to another since they depend on morphological and syntactic markings, and a single language may not mark all of them. Tense and aspect are among the crucial categories upon which the distinction between the bands are made. Other properties include case roles and modality. The verbs ranked in (161) are those in main and coordinate clauses. A script-determined action sequence in Band 7 is a sequence of events/actions that collocate by virtue of being in the same frame, i.e., events that nearly always go together. The verb classes (inherent aspect) comprise statives and nonstatives, i.e., events/actions/activities.

---

[41]However, many studies have shown that even in languages where this tendency holds, the perfective may also occur in the background, while the imperfective may also occur in the foreground (Waugh 1990, Rafferty 1979, Chvany 1990, Smith 1991).

[42]For detailed discussion of Longacre's verb ranking schema, see Longacre 1982 and 1989.

(161) Bands of salience in English narrative (from Longacre 1989:416)

Band 1   Past (S/Agent) action, (S/Agent/Patient) motion
Storyline   Past (S/Experiencer) Cognitive events (punctual adverbs)
            Past (S/Patient) contingencies

Band 2   Past Progressive (S/Agent) background activities
Background   Past (S/Experiencer) cognitive states (durative adverbs)

Band 3   Pluperfects (Events, activities out of sequence)
Flashback   Pluperfects (cognitive events/states out of sequence)

Band 4   Stative verbs/adjectival predicates/verbs with
                        inanimate subjects (descriptive)
Setting (expository) "Be" verbs/verbless clauses (equational)
                    "Be"/"Have" (existential, relational)

Band 5   Negatives
Irrealis (other possible Modals/futures
  words)

Band 6   Past tense (cf. setting)
Evaluation (author intrusion)   Gnomic present

Band 7   Script-determined
Cohesive band (verbs in   Repetitive
  preposed/postponed   Back reference
  adverbial clauses)

Longacre's verb ranking schema addresses most of the issues concerning foreground in the literature (see chapter 6). By the combination of properties, the schema presents the foreground/background distinction as a continuum rather than binary. It presents a gradation of verb forms, based on tense, aspect, and modality, from the most dynamic to the most static. His storyline (comparable to foreground) is a scalar cluster-concept consisting of punctual, sequential, transitive, volitional events, with a hierarchy of subjects: agent → experiencer → patient, i.e., from the most to the least salient. The rest of his schema presents varying degrees of backgrounding, from most dynamic to most static.

In summary, the foreground of the narrative discourse correlates with the past tense, perfective, and nonstative inherent aspects. Sequentiality, the most crucial property of the narrative foreground, is brought about by the presence of these aspectual qualities. All other tenses and aspectual values, which do not express sequentiality, characterize the background material. However, none of the works discussed above includes phasal aspect among the crucial properties of the narrative foreground.

My proposal in this chapter is that all three types of aspect, i.e., perfectivity, inherent, and phasal aspects, contribute to the foreground-background distinction in narrative discourse, as exemplified in Obolo.

7.2 The data

The data for this chapter consist of two narrative texts: Wandering Boy (WB), an oral text told by a woman of about forty-five years of age; and FIGHT, a first-person personal experience story of a fight between two brothers, told by a thirteen-year-old boy. Since the functions of tense and aspect are similar in the two texts, only the WB text is discussed in detail. Tables showing the distribution of aspect in the FIGHT story are given in §7.6.

The WB text is not a typical Labovian type of narrative (Labov 1972:363) in that it does not have all the parts of Labov's narrative schema which includes: abstract, orientation, complicating action, evaluation, result or resolution, and coda.[43] WB has no abstract, no evaluation, and no coda. It has an orientation and eight complicating-action-and-result episodes. Each interaction with people (or the bird) who use up something that the boy has comprises a complicating-action-and-result episode. Each episode consists of the boy's interaction with a different set of participants.

In the first episode, the boy enters the forest with a bow and arrows to shoot birds. In the second episode, a fish-trapper takes the boy's bird and gives him some crayfish. In the third episode, some anglers use up the boy's crayfish and give him some fish. In episode four, the maize eaters eat up the boy's fish and give him some maize. In episode five, the oil people eat up the boy's maize and give him a hoe. In episode six, the farmers take the boy's hoe and give him some yams. In episode seven, a cow eats up the boy's yams and its owners give the boy some articles of clothing. Finally in episode eight, a bird deceives the boy, collects his clothes, and flies away with them, and the boy goes back home crying.

7.3 The structure

As mentioned above, the text consists of a setting or orientation and eight episodes. The orientation and the episodes are listed in (162).

---

[43]To these, other scholars who have written about narrative discourse, like Longacre (1983), add the climax or peak, which is the highest point in the story or episode; and a denouement, which is an anticlimax that comes before the coda.

Tense and Aspect in Narrative Discourse

(162) Macro-structure of the Wondering Boy story

Orientation
Episode 1: boy and the bird
Episode 2: boy and the fish-trapper
Episode 3: boy and the anglers
Episode 4: boy and the maize eaters
Episode 5: boy and the oil people
Episode 6: boy and the farmers
Episode 7: boy and the cow
Episode 8: boy and the bird

At the end of each episode, the boy moves from one location to another where he meets a new set of participants. At the beginning of the next episode, dialogue begins between the boy and the new participants. A special set of sequential verb forms, *ni, neni,* Dstem (reduplication of the perfective verb stem), and *keki,* show a pattern that helps to define the structure of each episode. Almost as a rule, every episode, except the last one, begins with a simplex *(ni)* inchoative verb and ends with the reduplicated *(neni)* inchoative verb. Each episode has some specially reduplicated verbs, Dstem, in between. The last episode, which does not fit this pattern, starts and ends with Dstem verbs. This nonuniformity of the last episode singles it out as special. As an illustration, the setting and episode 2, a typical episode, are discussed below.

The orientation. The orientation starts with a formulaic clause which sets the time frame as a fictional distant past and describes the location of the story. This is followed by the introduction of the protagonist, the boy, and an action which he performed. The entire orientation is given in (163). Apart from one occurrence of *ni* in (d), none of the special verb forms described above is found in the orientation. This peculiar occurrence of *ni* in the orientation is discussed in §7.5.

(163) a. *ámà   ó-nàñá   í-kwéék*
 town 3sg-depart NSP-stay
 Once, there was a town.

 b. *m̀gbọ̀ ámà ó-nàñá   í-kwéék*
 time town 3sg-depart NSP-stay
 When the town was there

 c. *í-kààñ   gwúñ   èbíríéèñ gê*
 3sg-have child male   one
 there was a boy

d. ò-**nî-mọ̀nọ́**   òràáñ
   3SG-INCH-take arrows
   who took (his bow and) arrows

e. *í-jé   í-nííñ   órôn*
   NSP-walk NSP-enter forest
   (and) went into the forest

f. *í-sí   í-wèék   òfût*
   NSP-go NSP-look^for bird
   to look for birds (to shoot).

Episode 2. Episode 2 starts with an orientation in which the new participant, the fish-trapper, is introduced. The trapper's first action is expressed with *ni*, and the boy's response with *neni*. The trapper's subsequent response is a twin action, a speech followed by an action, and these are expressed with a Dstem and a *ni*, respectively. Then the boy's final response is expressed with a *neni* verb. Tense is nonfuture throughout.

The orientation of this episode describes the time and location of the episode, and also introduces the new participant, the fish-trapper, and the background activity she was involved in. In terms of tense and aspect, it contains a verbless stative clause followed by an imperfective relative clause with an activity verb, which describes what the trapper was doing. This is given in (164).

(164) a. *mgbọ̀ yà   ògwú òkêt   gê mé òkólò yà*
         time DDEMS^g DET^sg fish^trap one PREP creek DDEM^sg
         At that time, there was a fish-trapper in that creek

   b. *ó-ké-bé   í-kwọ̀kọ́   òkêt*
      3SG-IMPF-REL NSP-fishing fish^trap
      fishing with (her) fish trap.

The trapper's initial action, a complicating incident, contains a perfective *ni* inchoative achievement verb in the main clause, followed by a perfective accomplishment verb in the coordinate clause. These are given in (165).

(165) a. *ògwú òkêt   yà   ó-**ní-múñ**   òfût yà*
         DET^sgfish^trap DDEM^sg 3SG-INCH-spot bird DDEM^sg
         The trapper spotted the bird

   b. *mè   í-mọ̀nọ́*
      CONJ NSP-take
      and took (it).

The boy's response to the trapper's initial action comprises a step toward the resolution of the complication. The main clause in the response contains a perfective *neni* inchoative verb. The entire response is given in (166).

(166) a. gwúñ yà   ó-!nê-nĭ-tét   ògwú òkêt   yì
         child DDEM^sg 3SG-REDUP-INCH-hold DET^sg fish^trap PDEM^sg
         The boy held the trapper

   b. í-bé   í-nyî   ọ̀mộ òfùt kàñ
      NSP-say 3SG^HORT-give 3SG bird 3SG^POSS
      asking her to give him his bird.

The trapper's second response to the boy contains what may be considered to be the climax of the episode. She reciprocates by giving the boy some of the crayfish she has caught. In terms of the special verb forms, this response contains a Dstem and a *ni* verb form. The response is given in (167).

(167) a. ògwú òkêt   ó-!bê-bè
         DET^sg fish^trap 3SG-REDUP-say
         The fish trapper said

   b. mè í-nĭ-gwọ́   èsé   î-kwọ̀kọ́-bé   mé lék òkêt
      CONJ NSP-INCH-scoop crayfish 3SG-fished-REL PREP body fish^trap

      í-sà   í-nyí   gwújà yà
      NSP-take NSP-give child DDEM^sg
      and scooped some crayfish which she caught with the fish trap, (and) gave it to the boy.

The boy's final response, given in (168), is a kind of denouement to the episode. The main clause in the response contains the *neni* inchoative verb form in (a). The repetition of the verb in (b) marks durativity.

(168) a. gwúñ yà   ó-nê-nĭ-bọ̀kọ́   èsé   yà
         child DDEM^sg 3SG-REDUP-INCH-receive crayfish DDEM^sg
         Then the boy received the crayfish

   b. mè   í-sà   í-jé   í-jé   í-jé   í-jé
      CONJ NSP-take NSP-walk NSP-walk NSP-walk NSP-walk
      and walked, and walked, and walked, with it

c. mè í-sí í-múñ ògbògbò ǹsàbón íriééñ ògbò kàñ
   CONJ NSP-go NSP-see many   children male mates 3sg^POSS
   and saw many young men like himself

d. é-kwéék-bé í-kí-tó   úkǫ́ǫ́k
   cpl-sit-REL NSP-IMPF-cast hook
   sitting, (and) angling.

7.4 Special narrative verb forms

In my database, there are certain verb forms that occur in the narrative (WB) and also in the procedural texts, but not in any other discourse genre. These special verb forms include the reduplication of the inchoative affix *ni* to *neni*, the imperfective *ki* to *keki*, and the reduplication of the perfective verb stem (Dstem). All of these reduplications have a special tone pattern of down-stepped fall, i.e., a fall from down-stepped high to low, on the reduplicated syllable, as illustrated in (169).

(169) Special narrative verb forms

    Inchoative: **neni** as in *í-!nê-nǐ-bén*
                              3sg-REDUP-INC-carry
                              (then) s/he carried

    Perfective: **Dstem** as in *í-!bê-bèn*
                                3sg-REDUP-carry
                              (and/then) s/he carried

    Imperfective: **keki** as in *í-!kê-kǐ-bén*
                                3sg-REDUP-IMPF-carry
                              (and/then) s/he was carrying

The distribution of these forms in four sample texts in the database, a narrative (WB), a procedural (FISH), an expository compare-and-contrast (PROGS), and a hortatory (WARN) text, is given in (170).

(170) Distribution of the special narrative forms

Text	neni	keki	Dstem
WB	16	3	25
FISH	3	0	2
PROGS	0	0	1
WARN	0	0	0

As (170) shows, the special forms only occur in narrative and procedural texts, in which sequentiality is a crucial factor. The one Dstem verb that occurs in the PROGS text is found in an embedded narrative paragraph in the text. This distribution confirms that these are special verb forms that mark sequentiality and only occur in sequential discourse.

These verb forms have four properties. First, they do not occur paragraph-initially. They are totally dependent on preceding events, and therefore may be said to be anaphoric in nature. A listener hearing any of these verb forms would want to know what happened before. Secondly, in my database, they all occur only with agentive subjects, not experiencer or patient subjects. Thirdly, they are all found in main clauses, not in paratactic or coordinate clauses. In a main clause that involves a serial verb construction, they occur in the first verb slot. Where this slot is occupied by a modifying verb, then the modifying verb takes on the special form. Fourthly, in the narrative, they are nearly always associated with change of subject, or resumption of plot action, where the subject remains the same. In the procedural texts, they are always associated with change of steps. Their distribution in the narrative text is given in (171). Their distribution in procedural discourse is discussed in chapter 8. In the three examples (two for Dstem, one for *keki*) in (171) where a special form occurs twice consecutively with the same subject, the second occurrence is used to reestablish the storyline after a long interruption by a speech.

(171) Special verbs as markers of change of subjects

	new subject		old subject		Total
Dstem	24	92%	2	8%	26
neni	16	100%	0	0%	16
keki	2	67%	1	33%	3

To understand how these special forms function in the text, especially the Dstem and *neni* forms which are both perfective, i.e., to know when one is used rather than the other, foreground parameter of unexpectedness is used. A chart of the relational structure of the WB text reveals that the Dstem and *keki* forms tend to be used for events that express expected response to stimuli, while the *neni* forms tend not to occur in this context. This is illustrated in (172) and (173) where (a) is the stimulus and (b) the response.

(172) a. *í-!nê-nǐ-sà   àchá yà   í-nyí*
3sg-REDUP-INC-take hoe DDEM^sg NSP-give
(Then) he gave the hoe (to the people)

  b. *ífè chà é-!sâ-sà àchá yà í-gbọ́ úkó*
   people DDEM^pl CPL-REDPI-take hoe DDEM^sg NSP-weed farm
   (and) those people used the hoe to weed their field.

(173) a. *í-kpộ-kpọ̀k í-bén í-wùlú*
    3SG-REDUP-ITER NSP-carry NSP-fly
    As soon as it flew off again,

  b. *gwúñ yà ó-!kê-kǐ-kọ́t*
   child DDEM^sg 3SG-REDUP-IMPF-sing
   the boy (began and continued) to sing.

The distribution of the special verb forms as responses and nonresponses to stimuli in the WB text is given in (174).

(174) Use of special narrative verb forms

Form	response		nonresponse	
neni	1	6%	15	94%
Dstem	21	81%	5	19%
keki	3	100%	0	0%

Of the five times that Dstem is used in nonresponse expressions, three instances are expected in other ways unrelated to response. Two of them, exemplified in (175) and (176), are expected outcomes of the given situations, while the third one, exemplified in (177), is an expected response to a visually observed situation.

In example (175), a cow eats up the boy's yams, and the boy catches the cow. Then the owners of the cow buy a lot of clothes for the boy as compensation for his yams. The boy trying on the clothes is an expected next step in the situation.

(175) *í-!kpû-kpùlù ḿkpọ́ kàñ chì í-tàp mé lék*
   3SG-REDUP-gather thing 3SG^POSS PDEM^pl NSP-put PREP body
   He gathered these his things (clothes) (and) put them on (his) body.

In (176), a bird called *Ǹkọ̀nkọ̀* tricks the boy and collects all his clothes. So the boy, lamenting, put his hands on his head and went home crying. In the culture, this action is not an unexpected outcome of a bad situation.

(176) gwúñ yà   ó-!bê-bènè   úbọ́k íbà   í-tòóñ   mé íbòt
       child DDEM^sg 3sg-REDUP-lift hand two NSP-place PREP head
       The boy placed (his) two hands on (his) head

In (177), the boy walks off with his hoe and sees some farmers weeding in their fields with sticks. He asks them, "How are you weeding your fields?" Since he has the missing instrument, the hoe, and it is his habit to give things to people to help them accomplish their goals, his question is an expected response to the problem of the farmers, which he sees.

(177) í-!bê-bè   úkó ènyì é-kí-gbộ-gbọ̀   yê
       3sg-REDUP-say farm 2pl cpl-IMPF-REDUP-weed   QUES
       He said, "How are you weeding the farm?

With these three examples shown to be expected, the percent expectedness of Dstem is increased from 81% to 92%, while the level of unexpectedness is reduced to 8%.

The remaining two uses of Dstem for nonresponse (and therefore unexpected) expressions occur consecutively in the last episode, and in totally unexpected contexts. In the first context, Dstem is used to introduce the participant ǹkọ̀nkọ̀, the bird, who eventually flies off with the boy's clothes. Other participants are introduced with ordinary nonspecial perfective verb forms. Immediately following this occurrence, another Dstem verb is used to initiate a conversation between the boy and ǹkọ̀nkọ̀, a function that is undertaken by ni or neni everywhere else in the story. These uses, along with other things, probably point to the fact that this may be the most salient paragraph in the story, that is, the climax. These two unexpected uses of Dstem are given in (178) and (179).

(178) ǹkọ̀nkọ̀   ó-!nâ-nàñà   í-sìbí   í-nú
       Nkonko 3sg-REDUP-depart   NSP-come^out   NSP-come
       Nkonko appeared (and) came (to the boy).

(179) gwúñ yí   ó-!tû-tùmù   í-nyí   ǹkọ̀nkọ̀   í-bé
       child PDEM^sg 3sg-REDUP-speak   NSP-give Nkonko   NSP-say
       This boy spoke to Nkonko, saying...

In the same way as the unexpected uses of Dstem may say something about the paragraph in which they occur, the one use of neni form in an expected response context can be said to imply something about the episode in which it occurs. Its use in a response position in episode one may be a pointer to the introductory nature of the episode. The neni verb form, as (174) confirms, is used to express unexpected nonresponse events. But in

(180) it expresses an expected response, a function that is normally expressed by Dstem forms. Here the boy had shot at a bird, which instinctively ran towards a creek, and the boy ran after it. The boy running after the bird he had shot is expected, but it is expressed instead with *neni*.

(180) gwúñ yà   ó-!nê-nǐ-gòọ́k
       child DDEM^sg   3sg-REDUP-INC-follow
       Then the boy went after (it).

The uses of the special forms in terms of expectedness is shown in (181). While *neni* forms are used to express unexpected events, the Dstem and *keki* forms express pragmatically expected events. The *keki* forms express pragmatically expected durative events.

(181) Expectedness of the special verb forms

Form	Expected		Unexpected	
neni	1	6%	15	94%
Dstem	24	92%	2	8%
keki	3	100%	0	0%

These special verb forms arise as a special means of marking sequentiality. This is accomplished by reduplicating the aspectual morphemes, and it is done in a special way, by a special tone pattern, to set them apart from other reduplications. While *neni* is the special reduplication of the inchoative morpheme *ni*, *keki* is the special reduplication of the imperfective morpheme *ki*. Since the perfective has no overt morphological marking, the verb stem is reduplicated in the same way as the other aspectual morphemes, with the same tone pattern. This gives rise to the Dstem form. On the basis of this, the Dstem form may also be said to be aspectual.

7.5 Grounding in the narrative discourse

All supportive material in the WB text is background material. It includes all orientations, whether at the beginning of the whole text or at the beginning of each episode. The background also includes all embedded speeches. Since this text is primarily an action text, the speeches only function as supportive material to explain the events. Supportive material also includes most explanations and descriptions in the body of the text. These are expressed by complement, hypotactic, and relative clauses. The table in (182) shows the foreground/background distinction in terms of clause types and mode. Speeches are not included in the table. Main and coordinate clauses tend to be foreground material, while relative and hypotactic clauses tend to be background material. In the same way, irrealis clauses tend to be background material.

However, 4 (11%) of the irrealis clauses occur in the foreground in this text. These are four negative statements that express occasions when the people who used up the boy's things refused to give him anything in return. These negative statements keep the story going. Without them, there would be no story. It is not strange to have negatives in the foreground. Negatives which are essential to the plot of the story are justifiably considered foreground events (Fleischman 1985).

(182) Distribution of clause types and modes

Clauses

	main		coord		para		comp		relative		hypo	
FG	73	94%	12	75%	7	64%	37	64%	1	16%	0	
BG	5	6%	4	25%	4	36%	21	36%	5	84%	6	100%

Modes

	realis		irrealis	
FG	110	58%	4	11%
BG	81	42%	32	89%

Another unusual property shown in the table is the presence of an embedded relative clause in the foreground. In describing the protagonist in this story, one thing that is said about him marks the beginning of the plot of the story. This is that he took his bow and arrows and went into the forest to look for birds to shoot. As discussed in the next section, this relative clause also contains a typical foreground temporal property, the inchoative aspect marking *ni*, which expresses sequentiality. Because it initiates the plot of the story and is specially marked for sequentiality, this embedded relative clause belongs in the foreground. The clause complex in which this occurs is given in (183).

(183) a. *î-kààñ   gwúñ èbíriééñ gê*
       3sg-have child male   one
       There was a boy

   b. *ò-nî-mǫ̀nǫ́   òràáñ*
       3sg-INCH-take arrows
       who took (his bow and) arrows

c. í-jé   í-níñ   órôn
   NSP-walk NSP-enter forest
   (and) went into the forest

d. í-sí   í-wèék   òfũt
   NSP-go NSP-look^for bird
   to look for birds (to shoot).

The difference between foreground and supportive background material is illustrated in episode 8, which is given in (184) and (185). While (184) exemplifies the background, (185) exemplifies the foreground material. (Numbers in brackets are the clause numbers of the original WB text.)

(184) WB episode 8 (background)

[164] únékwùñ kpô-nŭ
      friend, look

[165] ìrè ḿkpọ́ yí îgbĕ èmì yê
      whether these things suit me

[167] îyàk
      wow!

[168] ké ìgbĕ òwù
      they suit you

[169] ngwà nyî ọ́mộ
      now, give them to me

[170] íyákà ítâp-nŭ
      to also wear

[171] mè òwù kpọ̀
      and you look

[172] mè môgbè ọ́mộ
      whether they will suit me

[173] ìké îgbè-bé òwù
      as they suit you

[177] ínàñá mé ìjọ̀ñ
      away from the ground

Tense and Aspect in Narrative Discourse

[178] ífó ìnyòn̄
go up

[183] íkpôkpòk íbén íwúlú
as soon as it flew off

[187] ìkâyáká ìsǎ ìnú
it did not bring them back

[189] mè íkító ító
and he was crying

[190] íkíjé úkpók úbók ífó
(and) returning home empty-handed

(185) WB episode 8 (foreground)

[160] ǹkònkò ónânàn̄à ísìbí
Nkonko appeared

[161] ínú
(and) came

[162] gwún̄ yí ótútùmù ínyí ǹkònkò
the boy spoke to Nkonko

[163] íbé
(and) said

[166] ǹkònkò óbêbè
Nkonko said

[174] í!nênǐbén ḿkpó chà
then it took those things

[175] ítàp
(and) put them on

[176] mè íwùlú íbéné
and flew up

[179] gwún̄ yà ó!kêkǐkót
the boy (resumed) singing

[180] ǹkọ̀nkọ̀ óyâyàkà íwùlú
Nkonko again flew (down)

[181] ínísọ̀ọ́k
(and) came (and) landed

[182] mè íyáká íkpọ́k bén íwùú
and flew off again

[184] gwùñ yà ó!kêkĩkọ́t
the boy (resumed) singing

[185] òsô m̀gbọ̀ ítá ǹkọ̀nkọ̀ ósâsà ḿkpọ́ chà mé lék
the third time, Nkonko took those things on its body

[186] íwùlú íchép
(and) flew off

[188] gwùñ yà óbêbènè ùbọ́k íbà ítòóñ mé íbòt
the boy put (his) two hands on (his) head

It is clear from these examples that the plot of the story in episode 8 is carried by the clauses in example (185), the foreground, while those in example (184) only provide supportive material. Example (185) tells what happened to the boy, what the boy did, and what ǹkọ̀nkọ̀ the bird did.

In summary, the narrative foreground consists of material that advances the plot of the story, while the background consists of material that does not advance the plot. Background material may include embedded speeches in an action narrative, as well as explanations and descriptions, and irrealis clauses. However, the analysis of this story has suggested that certain irrealis and embedded relative clauses may be foregrounded when they are essential to the movement of the plot of the story.

7.6 Tense and aspect in narrative grounding

The WB story is told in past time. The temporal frame is given in the setting, and every temporal reference within the story takes its orientation from that. In this case, the temporal setting is the distant past, a formulaic temporal setting that is used in all folktales. This time reference is used all through the foreground, as well as in most background material. The future and tense-neutral generic expressions are found only in the background in embedded speeches.

Tense and Aspect in Narrative Discourse 93

The distribution of aspect in the foreground and background in the WB text is given in (186)-(187). The tables reveal certain characteristic patterns in the use of the different aspectual distinctions in narrative grounding. The figures in (186) are represented in percentages in (187).

(186) Distribution of aspect in WB foreground and background

	Perfective		Inherent				Phasal					
	PFTV	IMPF	STA	ACT	ACC	ACH	INC	CMPL	DUR	ITER	IMM	INCH
FG	109	4	0	37	46	9	2	4	4	3	0	32
BG	31	16	8	14	9	3	0	1	0	0	2	2
Total	140	20	8	51	55	12	2	5	4	3	2	34

(187) Distribution of aspect in WB foreground and background by percentage

	Perfective		Inherent				Phasal					
	PFTV	IMPF	STA	ACT	ACC	ACH	INC	CMPL	DUR	ITER	IMM	INCH
FG	78	20	0	73	84	75	100	80	100	100	0	94
BG	22	80	100	27	16	25	0	20	0	0	100	6

In addition to Hopper's (1979) proposal that there is a correlation between the perfective and the foreground and Dry's (1981) proposal of a correlation between nonstativity and the foreground, I add a third correlation, that is between the inchoative and the foreground. The inchoative implies a change of state, an important element in sequentiality, which, in turn, is crucial in narrative foreground. In this way, the three aspectual distinctions contribute to the narrative foreground.

Specifically, the data reveal that in the distribution of aspect in narrative grounding, the perfective (perfectivity) and the inchoative (phasal) predominantly occur in the foreground, while the imperfective (perfectivity), the stative (inherent), and the phasal immediative (because of its unique property of reiterating already given information) predominantly occur in the background. Also, all nonstative inherent aspects, as well as the rest of the phasal aspects (i.e., inceptive, completive, durative, and iterative), though infrequent, tend to occur in the foreground.

However, as the table in (188) shows, there are four imperfectives in the foreground. These are the special reduplicated *keki* forms, which may be called promoted imperfectives. This special reduplicated form is promoted in that, here an imperfective form which is normally used in the background is used here in a context which is normally foreground. All other occurrences of the imperfective are found in the background.

The occurrence of the simple imperfective in the background only, and not also in the foreground, has an important implication. Dry (1981), in her discussion of foreground, concludes that change of state, not perfectivity, is the crucial factor in narrative time shift. Activities, accomplishments, and achievements all involve change of state. But when they occur with the simple nonpromoted imperfective, they fail to shift the narrative time, and are therefore backgrounded. When they occur with perfective, they advance narrative plot, and are therefore foregrounded.

To the extent that perfectivity does not make states into foreground material, and nonstativity, which implies change of state, does not make unpromoted imperfectives into foreground material, it is clear that the crucial factor in narrative time shift is neither change of state alone nor perfectivity alone, but perfectivity plus change of state. Perfectivity and change of state are two important and interactive components in the expression of sequentiality.

This makes sense in view of the fact that two types of aspect are involved in their discussion, and each contributes independently to foregrounding. The distribution of perfective states and imperfective nonstates in terms of grounding is given in (188) to illustrate this fact. The third type of aspect, phasal aspect, also contributes to grounding as has been discussed already.

(188) Perfective states and imperfective nonstates in WB

	FG		BG		Total
Perfective states	0	0%	6	100%	6
Imperfective nonstates	4	25%	12	75%	16
Perfective nonstates	87	86%	14	14%	101

In the WB text, all the imperfective nonstates are activities and, as shown in (188), all the four foregrounded imperfective nonstates are promoted imperfectives. The fourteen backgrounded perfective nonstates consist of complement, relative, and hypotactic clauses, which are nearly all background material in my database. The table, therefore, shows that all perfective states and all unpromoted imperfective nonstates are background elements, the reason being that they do not express sequentiality.

The distribution of aspect in the FIGHT text is given in (189)–(191). The percentage distribution of the crucial aspects (i.e., perfective and inchoative in the foreground, and imperfective and states in the background) in FIGHT, shown in (190), is very similar to the one in WB. In the same way, the distribution of the different aspectual combinations in FIGHT, given in (191), is very similar to the ones in WB. In terms of tense, like the WB story, the FIGHT story is told in the nonfuture time. The figures in (189) are represented in percentages in (190).

(189) Distribution of aspect in FIGHT foreground and background

	Perfective		Inherent				Phasal				
	PFTV	IMPF	STA	ACT	ACC	ACH	INC	CMPL	DUR	ITER	IMM	INCH
FG	38	2	0	20	9	11	1	0	0	0	0	7
BG	22	4	7	14	3	2	0	0	0	0	0	0
Total	60	6	7	34	12	13	1	0	0	0	0	7

(190) Distribution of aspect in FIGHT foreground and background by percent

	Perfective		Inherent				Phasal				
	PFTV	IMPF	STA	ACT	ACC	ACH	INC	CMPL	DUR	ITER	IMM	IMM
FG	63	33	0	59	75	85	100	0	0	0	0	100
BG	37	63	100	41	25	15	0	0	0	0	0	0

(191) Perfective states and imperfective nonstates in FIGHT

	FG		BG		Total
Perfective states	0	0%	7	100%	7
Imperfective nonstates	2	29%	5	71%	7
Perfective nonstates	38	72%	15	28%	53

In summary, the narrative texts in my database are told in the nonfuture time, and this is the time reference that occurs in the foreground. The future tense, and overt expressions of the remote past are found in the background. All the three aspectual distinctions contribute to the foreground/background distinction in narrative discourse. The foreground tends to consist mostly of the perfective (perfectivity), inchoative (phasal), and nonstative (inherent) aspects. These are aspectual combinations that express sequentiality. Under certain circumstances, promoted imperfectives may also occur in the foreground. The background tends to consist mostly of the imperfective (perfectivity), statives (inherent), and immediative (phasal).

7.7 The concept of a scalar continuum

The major issues in the literature concerning foreground and background are: (1) that the foreground is a cluster concept rather than a one component concept, (2) that the foreground/background distinction is a scalar continuum rather than a binary opposition, and (3) that the foreground is absolute in nature in discourse analysis discussion, and relative in literary criticism. Of these three issues, the most problematic one seems to be the second, i.e., that the parameters that indicate grounding in discourse, rank on a scale of graded salience from most foregrounded to most backgrounded.

In this study, for purposes of presentation and analysis, the foreground and background are presented in a way that seems to make them play off each other as a binary opposition. In reality this is not the case. Also, it seems to be the case that in identifying grounding in discourse, the real substantive issue is to define and identify the foreground, and everything else is background after that.

One cannot overlook the practical fact, however, that certain foreground properties are more salient than others in advancing the plot of a narrative. The defining properties of transitivity, for example, are discourse-determined, and its parameters can be ranked from highest to lowest based on the facet of effectiveness or intensity with which the action is transferred from one participant to another. Then each of the parameters has a high component as well as a low component based on the same effectiveness factor. From this, it appears that high transitivity correlates with foregrounding, and low transitivity with backgrounding. Going by these correlations, it follows that the higher transitivity parameters are higher foregrounding parameters than the lower ones. Stretching this further, the high component of the highest ranking parameter correlates with the highest level foreground, while the low component of the lowest parameter correlates with the lowest level background. Therein lies the concept of scalar continuum in the distinction of the foreground and the background. The same principle can be applied to actual discourse, where the components of the texts are arranged in order of their salience in advancing the plot of the story, i.e., in the order that depicts a progressive departure from the main line of the story. The table in (192) is supposed to represent the same concept in the present study.

One of the questions that can be asked is how the different degrees of the foreground serve the communication purpose of the speaker, and whether or not all these different degrees serve to advance the flow of discourse, and provide the backbone of the discourse. No communication is without a purpose, and grammatical structures of the text are selected by the speaker or writer to convey his message. Also, all aspects of the speaker's message do not have equal prominence. Therefore, in conveying his message, he carefully selects his verbal forms depending on his assessment or awareness of his audience and the relative prominence of a particular aspect of the message. In the same way, since not all aspects of the gist (foreground) of the message the speaker intends to communicate have equal prominence, the speaker selects different verbal forms to convey the different degrees of prominence of his message. Therefore, the concept of scalar continuum does not just originate from the grammatical correlates of the foreground, such as, transitivity, aspect, tense, or clause type, but rather it originates directly from the communicative intention of the speaker. It is necessitated by the message itself and is not just a product of the verbal forms the speaker selects to convey his message.

The answer to the last part of the question (i.e., whether or not all the different degrees of foreground serve to advance the flow of discourse) would be that some degrees of foreground advance the flow of discourse and provide the backbone of the discourse more (or less) than others, given the degree of prominence of the message they encode.

One of the crucial questions that the concept of a scalar continuum inevitably invokes is at what point on the continuum does some item become contrastive with the background, that is, become foreground? The very nature of a scalar continuum presupposes a fuzzy middle between two extreme poles. This question is essentially insisting that the foreground/background distinction is a binary opposition as opposed to a continuum. It is asking for the dividing line between foreground and background. In practice, it is difficult to draw the dividing line.

The problem seems to be terminological, as in all probability there are varying degrees of foreground, i.e., from components that advance the narrative plot most to those that do not advance it at all. This affirms the concept of a scalar continuum, and effectively eliminates the foreground/background dichotomy. However, in the absence of a better terminology, foreground and background are used here.

In the context of the present work, another question that is obviously answered in the course of the study, but still needs to be addressed pointedly is why the concept of scalar continuum is important in understanding the function of tense and aspect in discourse. Tense and aspect are among the parameters by which grounding in discourse is defined. They help to shape the structure of the discourse genre by their contribution to the nature of foreground and background of the genre. This contribution includes the definition of the degrees of salience of foreground material in the formation of a particular discourse genre. For instance, the unexpected nonfuture perfective nonstative special inchoative verb in the main clause is more salient in advancing the plot of the narrative than the future stative verb. These two components represent the two ends of the continuum, the most foregrounded and the most backgrounded. The non inchoative nonfuture perfective verb in the main clause still advances the narrative plot, but it is not as salient as its inchoative counterpart. Also, the foreground nonfuture perfective inchoative verb in the main clause is not as salient as the nonfuture perfective special inchoative in the same environment. In the same way, if the realis nonfuture stative verb does not advance the narrative plot, the irrealis future stative verb does so even less (both are background material, the latter being more so than the former).

7.8 Summary

A typical narrative episode in Obolo is marked by the presence of special sequential verb forms. As the WB text shows, the foreground tends to consist mostly of nonfuture, realis, main, and coordinate clauses, while the background tends to consist mostly of irrealis, hypotactic, and embedded relative clauses. Some background material may also be in the past time reference, but in addition to this, other tenses such as future and remote past tend to only occur in the background. In special circumstances, embedded relative clauses and irrealis clauses may also occur in the foreground.

All types of aspect, i.e., perfectivity, inherent, and phasal aspects, contribute to the foreground/background distinction in narrative. The foreground tends to consist of perfective, inchoative, nonstative, while the background tends to consist of the imperfective, stative, and immediative.

The properties of the foreground mentioned in the literature include sequentiality and unexpectedness. A combination of these two properties gives a continuum, from most foregrounded to most backgrounded, along which the different foreground and background properties are placed. This continuum, based on the WB and FIGHT texts in my database, is given in (192).

The continuum nature of the foreground/background distinction is seen in the existence of two extreme poles and some in-between forms. There are certain properties, e.g., perfective inchoative, and perfective Dstem forms, that are typically foreground forms, and certain properties, e.g., simplex imperfective, immediative forms, and states, that are typically background forms. In between these two poles are the other perfective forms which occur in the background, and the promoted imperfective forms which occur in the foreground.

In (192) tense as a property is difficult to arrange in the continuum. Both nonfuture and future apply all through the continuum. Nonfuture unexpected special inchoative verb in the main clause is the foreground component with the highest salience, while the future stative verb in the hypotactic clause is the background component with the lowest salience.

Tense and Aspect in Narrative Discourse 99

The foreground is a cluster concept consisting of temporal and nontemporal properties, and not all of them are necessary for the definition of the foreground.

(192) Properties of foreground and background in WB and FIGHT texts

FG	Tense	Key Aspect	Form	Expected	Other properties
FG	nonfuture	special INCH	*neni*	unexpected	sequential, main
		other INCH	*ni*	unexpected,	sequential, main/ coordinate
		special PFTV	Dstem	expected,	sequential, main
		special IMPF	*keki*	expected,	nonsequential, main
		other PFTV	—	—	sequential, main/ coord/para
		other PFTV	—	—	sequential, hypo, rel cls
		IMM	—	—	sequential, hypo
		other IMPF	*ki*	—	nonsequential, any clause
BG	future	states	—	—	nonsequential, any clause

Regarding the argument over the foreground/background distinction being absolute or relative in nature, the overlapping properties discussed above makes the distinction clearly nonabsolute. What this shows is that even in the context of discourse analysis, where overt marking or stable identification of the foreground is emphasized, the foreground/background distinction may still not be absolute.

8
Tense and Aspect in Procedural Discourse

The structure of procedural discourse in Obolo comprises a string of paragraphs each with one or more subordinate consequential or conditional clause(s) followed by one or more main clause(s). Both sets of clauses may be elaborated. Usually, two types of paragraphs are employed. First the "what-to-have" paragraphs which describe the necessary prerequisites for the procedure. Immediately following these are the "what-to-do" paragraphs, the procedure itself. Introductions, opening and closing statements, and conclusions are not obligatory. Usually, the subject is in the second person for procedural with projection, and for the third person for procedural without projection.

The foreground in the procedural discourse also upholds the cluster concept nature of the definition of foreground. In terms of tense and aspect, the foreground of procedural discourse with projection consists, diagnostically, of future Dstem perfective (optional), inchoative, and inceptive verbs, while the foreground of the projectionless procedurals consists of all of the above except nonfuture rather than future tense. The procedural background, with or without projection, consists of nonfuture, imperfective, and stative verbs. Where there are inceptives, they usually encode foreground events. The foreground elements are all markers of sequentiality. Not all of them need to be present to identify an event as a foreground material. All other aspectual categories such as non-Dstem perfective, activities, accomplishments, and achievements may encode either foreground or background information.

8.1 The data

This chapter is based on four different texts. Two, written by two fourteen-year-olds, a boy and a girl, are taken from a children's magazine. The girl wrote an article on a dance group and the boy wrote one on fishing. These are subsequently referred to as DANCE and FISH, respectively. The third text on how to fire a cannon (referred to as CANNON) was recorded orally from a twenty-eight-year-old male teacher. The fourth text consists of two paragraphs taken from an oral expository text, FISH2,[44] told by a thirty-four-year-old man. In these paragraphs, the speaker tells how a particular kind of fishing net is made, not necessarily how to make it. This type of procedural discourse is described by Longacre (1983) as procedural without projection, i.e., without contemplation or anticipation that anybody will do it.

Regarding the nature of the texts, two of them, CANON and FISH, set out to describe procedures with projection, i.e., how to do it. But DANCE starts out as an expository discourse, describing a particular dance group, and ends up describing how the people in the group do their dancing. In the same way, the FISH2 paragraph is within the context of an expository discourse. While the first two texts employ the second person (plural in FISH, singular in CANON) as the predominant subject, DANCE and FISH2 are third-person procedural texts.

All the texts seem to be dominated by a particular structure, a consequential or conditional clause followed by a main clause, each with or without elaborations. This structure seems to be prototypical of procedural discourse in Obolo. Since a paragraph consists of a morphosyntactically marked group of clauses that together describe a topic or subtopic, and each step in the procedure describes a subtopic, the term "paragraph" in procedural discourse is used to refer to the consequential or conditional clause (with or without elaboration) and its main clause(s).

8.2 The structure

Charting the four texts, using the Callow and Callow (1992) text structure model, revealed the major sections or macro-structures in their hierachies. These are given in (193).

---

[44]Fishing 2 is one of the two expository texts on which chapter 10 on expository discourse is based. Only these two procedural paragraphs are discussed here; the rest are discussed in chapter 10.

(193) DANCE   FISH   CANON   FISH2

Introduction   —   Introduction   —
Procedure   Procedure   Procedure   Procedure
Coda   Coda   —   —

While all four texts have a procedure section, two have introductions and two have codas. These sections are discussed separately below in terms of tense and aspect. Occasionally, other characteristic structures are mentioned, but the emphasis is on tense and aspect. Because the procedure section is the largest and main part of the text, it is discussed last.

The introduction. In each introduction the topic of the text is introduced. While the introduction of the DANCE text introduces the dance group, who is involved, and what songs they sing, that of the CANON text introduces the two types of cannons, their use, and from what source the narrator knew how to shoot them. In terms of tense and aspect, both of the introductions are nonfuture and contain mostly nonsequential aspectual combinations, that is, perfective statives and imperfective nonstatives. A typical introduction is given in (194), taken from the first two sentences of the DANCE text.

(194) a. ífit álóm ìrè   ífit
       ifit alom 3sg-be play
       Ifit Alom is a dance group.

     b. èbíbáàñ é-kí-fit
        women cp-IMPF-play
        (That) women dance (in) (i.e., women's dance group).

     c. èmâ é-kí-kót   ókwà ùsém   òbòlò
        3pl cp-IMPF-sing song language Obolo
        They sing Obolo songs.

The coda. Two of the four texts have a concluding structure that very much resembles the Labovian type of coda which is normally found in narratives. According to Labov (1972) the coda, apart from signalling the end of the narrative, also contains general observations, or shows the effects of the events narrated on the narrator. Although coda is prototypically a part of the schema of the narrative discourse, the ones found in these clearly nonnarrative texts do seem to be performing the same functions. Actually, a coda is not necessary in a procedural discourse. Since it is not present in the CANON text told by the teacher who is an adult, one explanation may be that the fourteen-year-olds who wrote the texts with codas simply added them in the same way as they add morals to narratives. The codas are long and only relate loosely to the procedure described in the text.

In terms of tense and aspect, the coda may be future and/or nonfuture, and may have sequential and/or nonsequential aspectual combinations. The coda of the FISH text is given in (195) as an example. It is a recommendation by the narrator that every Obolo child should learn how to fish. In terms of tense and aspect, the coda of the FISH text is in the future tense, and the aspect of the independent verb, *mô-nwọ̀n* 'it will be good', is perfective stative which is a nonsequential aspectual combination.

(195) mô-nwọ̀n   í-bé   áyá   gwùñ   ò-nû   ìnyọ̀ñ   í-kwéèñ   úbọ́k
      3sg^FUT-good NSP-say new   child 3sg-come world   3sg-learn how

  é-kí-sí   m̀bọ́m
  cpl-IMPF-go   fishing

It would be good that a new child who comes into the world learns how to go fishing.

While some of these texts have introductions and codas, these two structures are, strictly speaking, not necessary parts of procedural discourse. The fact that they are not present in all four texts supports this conclusion. Therefore, these two features are considered background material in this genre.

The procedure. Of all the major sections or macro-structures in the texts, the procedure is the most complex. This section in each of the texts has a clearly distinguished bipartite structure, where the first part describes the major necessary equipment for the process, and the second describes the steps. These parts and their components are presented schematically in (196), and discussed separately.

(196) The procedure schema

		CANON	FISH	DANCE	FISH2
Equipment:		Opening	—	—	Opening
		List	List	List	List
What to do:		Opening	—	—	—
		Steps	Steps	Steps	Steps
		Conclusion	—	Conclusion	—

The equipment section consists of an optional opening statement followed by an obligatory listing of necessary equipment for the process.

Opening of equipment section. Following the introduction there is a statement which opens the description of the equipment section. In two of the four texts, CANON and FISH2, there is an opening statement which specifies the topic to be described in the text. The opening statements of these two texts are separate from the body of the text. In the other two texts, however, this is not the case. Rather, the first paragraph of the steps section is adapted to carry this introductory function. In terms of tense and aspect, the opening statements are nonfuture and have nonsequential aspectual combinations. The opening statement of the CANON text is exemplified in (197). It is nonfuture with perfective stative and habitual accomplishment aspectual combinations, both of which are nonsequential.

(197) ùbǫ́k é-kí-sà   í-sóók   ètîrìk   ì-rè
       how   cpl-IMPF-take NSP-shoot cannon   3sg-be
       The way to shoot cannon(s) is...

List of required equipment. The structure of this section differs slightly from text to text, but semantically each one describes the major things or qualifications which are necessary to have on hand before the process can be undertaken. The one in the CANON text specifies the type of cannon, a small one, and goes on to describe the two necessary pieces of equipment to have on hand, while that of the FISH text specifies some fishing materials. Also, the one in FISH2 lists physical equipment, i.e., three types of nets. But, rather than physical materials, as in all the other texts, the one in DANCE specifies membership in the dance group.

In terms of tense, while the equipment section in CANON, FISH, and DANCE texts are given in the future tense, the one in the FISH2 text is in the nonfuture. In terms of aspect, while the equipment section of CANON, FISH, and FISH2, which list the prerequisite materials, have nonsequential perfective states and imperfective nonstates, the same section in the DANCE text, which specifies membership, has sequential perfective activity. Two equipment paragraphs are given here to illustrate these properties. First, that of the FISH2 text, a nonfuture, nonsequential example is given in (198), then that of the DANCE text, a future sequential example is given in (199).

The FISH2 text does not have a separate equipment section. The equipment, in this case "about three kinds of nets," given in (198c), is rather tagged onto the first step as a summary. This first step is also different from other steps in that, rather than being sequential, it is described with a non sequential aspectual combination, which makes it more like an equipment-introducing clause.

(198) a. í-sĭ-chím
 3pl-CNS-sew
 Whenever they make it

b. é-kí-fièék   ńjìn mé èsêsé   chiéèñ
 cpl-IMPF-cut net PREP different mesh
 they cut different meshes of nets

c. ḿkpọ́ ò-bêt   lék   chiéèñ ńjìn ítá
 thing 3sg-resemble body mesh net three
 like three (different) meshes.

(199) èbí   gèèlék ì-bê-nùñ   mê-sì lék
 DETˆpl every 3pl-INT-enter cplˆFUT-go body
 All who want to join this dance group will go to

òg wù íbòt ífìt   yì   í-sí
DETˆsg head danceˆgroup PDEMˆsg NSP-go
the head of the group to

í-tàp   èriééñ kìbàñ
NSP-put name   3plˆPOSS
enroll themselves.

In this list of required equipment section, the difference in tense between the texts is significant. The tense established in this section runs all the way through the procedure and helps to determine the type of procedural discourse the particular text falls under. In Obolo the future tense marks a procedural discourse with projection, while the nonfuture marks a procedural discourse without projection. For a procedural text that has an introduction, the change in tense from nonfuture in the introduction to future in the required equipment section marks it as the beginning of the procedure proper. This is true of CANON and DANCE.

In terms of aspect, while the requirement sections of CANON, FISH, and FISH2 have perfective stative and habitual achievement, which are nonsequential aspectual combinations, that of the DANCE text contains a perfective activity which is a sequential aspectual combination. On the basis of aspects alone, this section in this text qualifies as a part of the steps in the procedure rather than as a part of the requirement section. But it is classified as belonging in the requirement section because, pragmatically, it takes place long before the dance and is not a part of the dancing procedure, which is described in the steps section.

Apart from tense and aspect, the structure of the requirement section differs from text to text. While CANON and DANCE have simple declarative statements, the same section in FISH and FISH2 consists of a combination of a condition or consequential clause followed by a main clause, a structure that characterizes procedural discourse. But in each of the two FISH texts, since this section describes equipment and contains nonsequential aspectual combinations which is not characteristic of the steps section, it is classified as describing equipment rather than describing steps. In two of the texts, CANON and FISH, this section, like the steps section, has second-person subjects, while DANCE and FISH2 have third-person subjects which also continue all through the steps section. In CANON, the person changes from third in the opening statement to second here. In none of the texts does this section have any formal conclusion or closure.

The "what-to-do" section as listed in (196) consists of three parts—two optional (opening and conclusion), and one obligatory (steps). These are discussed separately below.

The opening statement. In the CANON text, the what-to-do section starts with another opening statement. In this text, this statement clearly and effectively creates a demarcation between the equipment section and the procedure section by declaring the next step as the first thing to do. This is given in (200).

(200) òkpá-ótù ḿkpọ́ ó-bô-rọ̀   ì-rè
       first   thing   2sg-INT-do 3sg-be
       The first thing you will do is:

The procedural steps. The paragraphs in this part of each text, referred to henceforth as procedural paragraphs are markedly different from those in the other parts already discussed. Unlike the other sections, the procedural paragraphs consist almost entirely of a homogenous string of conditional clauses (the protasis), followed by consequence clauses (the apodosis), each with or without elaborations. The paragraphs in this section are different in terms of the aspectual marking on the verbs. Apart from the first or first two apodoses, all the verbs in the apodoses are specially marked for sequentiality by using the inchoative, simplex, or reduplicated, or by using the reduplicated verb stem. These verbs are stronger markers of sequentiality than the perfective alone. Since the verbs in the first step of each text are the initiators of the process, they do not have any special sequential marking. But other verbs do need this marking since it indicates that some steps have already been taken before the one in question, i.e., that the step in question depends on a previous one or previous ones.

In all the texts without opening statements, the procedural section begins with a consequential or conditional clause which introduces the topic of the section. While the one in FISH specifies evening fishing, the one in DANCE specifies the process of dancing in the particular dance group, and the one in FISH2 specifies the making of a particular type of net called *ǹkòtò*.

A typical first step, the one in FISH, is given in (201) to show the structure of a conditional clause followed by a main clause without any special sequential marking.

(201) a. *îré ènyì é-bê-sì   njin mé íkàkwùñ*
if   2pl cpl-INT-go net PREP evening
If you intend to go (fishing with a) net in the evening

b. *ènyì mê-dàsí   í-sí   í-tàp   njin mé újí   mé átásùk*
2pl cpl^FUT-first NSP-go NSP-put net PREP canoe PREP riverside
you will first go (and) put the net in the boat at the river.

After this first paragraph, the rest of the structure in the text consists of homogenous paragraphs each of which begins with a nonfuture consequential subordinate clause, followed by a main clause, each with or without modification(s). Each consequential clause recapitulates the previous step or provides another piece of assumed background information, while the main clause encodes the next step in the sequence. The main clause, which expresses the next step, is given in the future tense in procedurals with projection, and in nonfuture in procedurals without projection.

In this section, each of the four texts has an idiosyncratic characteristic in the main clauses. Among the three procedurals with projection, the CANON and FISH2 texts use the simplex *ni* inchoative in their main clauses, the FISH text uses the reduplicated *neni* inchoative, while the DANCE text uses the Dstem perfective. These verb forms are special markers of sequentiality, a crucial component in procedural discourse. The FISH2 text, which is a nonprojection procedural, uses the tense-neutral generic marker *rà*. A typical paragraph of each one of these texts is exemplified as follows, CANON in (202), FISH in (203), DANCE in (204), and FISH2 in (205).

(202) a. *ó-sĭ-gòn   ńtítààk yà   í-tàp   mé èmèn ètûrík*
2sg-CNS-push sand DDEM^sg NSP-put PREP inside cannon

í-sáñá
NSP-finish
When you finish pushing sand into the cannon,

b. òwù mô-**nǐ**-mònó ḿgbìdìm íbọ́k-ágbûrì
2sg 2sg^FUT-INCH-take portion gunpowder
you will then take a portion of gunpowder...

(203) a. mùñ í-sǐ-báák í-kèm mè ì-rè í-sǐ-tá
water 3sg-CNS-flow NSP-enough CONJ 3sg-be 3sg-CNS-ebb

í-kèm
NSP-enough
When the flow tide or ebb tide is just right,

b. ènyì mé-nê-**nǐ**-tééñ ùràñ
2pl CPL-REDUP-INCH-gather paddle(s)
you will then take paddles,

c. mè í-mònó éwòp mè ágòk
CONJ NSP-take scoop CONJ chewing^stick
and take a scoop (for bailing water) and some chewing sticks

d. í-tàp mé èmèn ókwùn
NSP-put PREP inside basket
(and) put (them) into a basket,

e. mè í-bén í-sìbí átásùk
CONJ NSP-carry NSP-go^out riverside
and carry (the basket) out to the riverside

f. í-sí í-tàp mé èmèn ùjí
NSP-go NSP-put PREP inside canoe
(and) put them in the boat.

(204) a. í-sǐ-jòp í-sáñá
3pl-CNS-dance NSP-finish
Whenever they finish dancing,

b. ògwú ísí mô-!**wû-wùt** òtítà kàñ
DET^sg front 3sg^FUT-REDUP-blow whistle 3sg^POSS
the leader will blow her whistle.

c. mê-!**fê-fìèèk** èyí kèyâ mè í-kọ́t òfífí
CPL-REDUP-stop DET^sg DDEM^sg CONJ NSP-sing another
They will stop that one and sing another.

(205) a. mè m̀gbọ̀ é-tàp ólík í-kàná mé ótú
PREP time cpl-put rope NSP-round PREP mouth
When they have put (a) rope around the opening

b. mî-rà í-ní-sà útì gê sǐ
cpl-GEN NSP-INCH-take stick one also
they would take a stick also

c. é-sà é-tòòñ mé ètétè kàñ
cpl-take cpl-place PREP middle 3sg^POSS
(and) they would place (it) in the middle of it

d. mè è-bộp
CONJ cpl-tie
and they would tie (it).

The statement of conclusion. Two of the four texts, DANCE and CANON, have formulaic conclusive statements that terminate the procedures. Since the FISH2 text discussed here is taken from the middle of an expository text, it does not have a terminal statement.

The terminal statement of the DANCE text is given in (206). This statement is a verbless stative main clause with a nonfuture habitual activity verb in the complement clause, which comes right after a future tense clause that describes the last step in the procedure. The anaphoric demonstrative, ìkéyà 'like that' refers back to the procedures just described, thus bringing the description to a close.

(206) ìkéyà ké èmâ é-kí-fìt ífìt álọ́m kìbàñ
like^that COMPL 3pl cpl-IMPF-play ifit alom 3pl^POSS
That is how they dance their Ifit Alom dance.

The terminal statement of the CANON text given in (207) also provides closure, in a similar manner, to the description of how to shoot a small cannon. The statement consists of a nonfuture perfective stative main clause verb with a habitual achievement verb in an embedded relative clause.

(207) a. éyí ì-rè úbọ́k
DEM^sg 3sg-be how
This is how

b. é-kí-sà í-sóók gwúñ ètîrík
cpl-IMPF-take NSP-shoot child cannon
(people) shoot small cannon(s).

Although two of the texts have closing statements, they are not necessary parts of the procedural discourse. Whenever they are found, they are characteristically nonfuture and have nonsequential aspectual combinations.

The special role of the inchoative in procedural discourse. The inchoative aspect is marked by two morphemes, *ni* and *-yákà*. While *ni* is used in contexts where sequentiality is of the essence, *-yákà* is used elsewhere. In all the texts except one, the inchoative morpheme *ni* is used to express sequentiality in accordance with this analysis.

However, in the CANON text, which also uses the *ni* inchoative for sequentiality, at some crucial point in the procedure there is a switch in the inchoative morpheme from *ni* to *yákà*. The procedure in this text is how to fire a cannon. Immediately after the last step is reached and the cannon sounds, the clean-up steps are expressed by means of *-yákà* rather than *ni*, which dominated all the steps before that point. The cannon sounding is expressed with an ordinary future without *ni*, probably since it is not a step to be performed by the human agent, but is rather a result of the agent's action. The main clauses that encode this information are given in (208) with the verb forms bolded.

(208) a. òwù **mô-nǐ-mọ̀nọ́** íbọ́k í-gìgéñé mé chiéèñ
        2sg 2sg^FUT-INCH-take gunpowder NSP-sprinkle PREP eye

        yà
        DDEM^sg
        You will then take some gunpowder (and) sprinkle (it) on the opening

    b. mè í-mọ̀nọ́ ùkáñ í-sà í-dá mé lék íkpá
        CONJ NSP-take fire NSP-take NSP-touch PREP body paper

        yà érè ó-gwòòk-bé íbọ́k-ágbûrì yà
        DDEM^sg place 2sg-pour-REL gunpowder DDEM^sg
        and touch the paper with fire (the paper) on which you poured the gunpowder.

    c. ọ̀mộ gáàlèk **mô-kùp** mé lék kàñ mè í-tààñ
        3sg alone 3sg^FUT-stay PREP body 3sg^POSS PREP NSP-sound
        It will stay (for a while) and sound by itself.

    d. mkpọ́ **ó-bô-yàkà** í-rọ́
        thing 2sg-INT-INCH NSP-do
        what you will then do (is)

e. òwù **mô-yàkà**   í-lìbí   í-fó   lék
   2sg 2sg^FUT-INCH NSP-run NSP-go^toward body
   you will then run back to it

f. òwù **mô-yàkà**   í-wèék   ḿkpọ́ gê í-sà   í-rọ̀kọ́
   2sg 2sg^FUT-INCH NSP-look^for thing one NSP-take NSP-dig^out

   ọ̀gọ́t í-sìbí   mé   ḭ̀jọ̀n̄
   3sg NSP-come^out PREP ground
   you will then look for something to dig it out of the ground.

Two factors may be responsible for the switch from *ni* to *yákà*. One may be sequentiality versus nonsequentiality as discussed in §5.5 where *ni* indicates sequence while *-yákà* does not indicate sequence. This means that in the text, after the goal of the procedure is reached, the sequentiality emphasis is switched off or ceases to matter. The steps are still arranged in sequence, but sequentiality is no longer crucial. The order of events from that point on is of no further significance. The second factor may be the difference between more important steps versus less important ones. The more important procedural steps are those that lead up to the goal of the procedure, and the less important steps are those that come after the goal has been reached. This importance seems to be connected with sequential order. To achieve the goal, it is important that the right order of the procedure be followed. After achieving the goal, it does not matter anymore what order things are cleaned up.

In summary, there are two types of procedural texts in Obolo, one with projection and the other without projection. The difference between them is the use of the future tense in the main clause of the one with projection and nonfuture tense in that of the projectionless one. Apart from these differences, a prototypical procedural text has a unique structure which consists of a subordinate consequential or conditional clause followed by an inchoative or Dstem main clause. While the subordinate clause recapitulates the previous step or introduces a necessary piece of assumed foreground information, the main clause expresses the step or steps in the procedure. The initial step does not need to be marked for sequentiality. But all other steps are sequential and are therefore marked for sequentiality using any of the sequential verb forms—inchoative *ni*, reduplicated inchoative *neni*, or special perfective reduplicated stem referred to in this study as Dstem. Formulaic opening and closing statements as well as introductions and codas may be present but are not obligatory.

8.3 Grounding in procedural discourse

In these texts all supportive materials are background information. These include the introduction, coda, and opening and terminal statements. The procedural paragraphs include the lists of equipment, subordinate consequential and conditional clauses, and all elaborations such as embedded relative clauses and complement clauses. All background material comments on, amplifies, and elaborates the foreground material. The background portions are mostly nonfuture in tense. Those that are expressed with the future tense include the equipment lists and some materials in the coda.

On the other hand, all the steps described in the text, without such elaborations as embedded relative clauses and complement clauses, are foreground materials. They are found in the steps section of each text, and they are mostly main, coordinate, and paratactic clauses. Where the step is expressed with a serial verb construction, all the verbs together form a part of the foreground. They constitute the essence or gist of the speakers' communicative goals. Without the background materials described above, these steps by themselves could convey, essentially, the gist of what the speakers intended to convey, whereas the background materials alone, without these steps, would not convey the gist of the speakers' goals. These facts are illustrated using the FISH text. First, the background material is given in (209), and the foreground material is given in (210). Numbers in square brackets indicate the clauses in the text.

(209) Introduction

[1]   săbùm òwù mónísìbí ótú újí m̀bọ́m èyí kwùñ,
Before you can be a fishing boat owner yourself,

[2]   òwù môdàsí íkááñ úràñ
you will first own a paddle

[3]   mè íkááñ sǐ éwòp
and also own a scoop.

[4]   săbùm òwù mó!nǐkááñ újí
Before you own a boat

[5]   òwù môkààñ sǐ ńjìn
you will also own a net.

Body

[6]   *iré ènyì ébêsì ńjìn mé íkàkwùñ*
        If you (pl) intend to go fishing in the evening

[9]   *ènyì ísĭtàp ńjìn ísáñá mé újí*
        when you finish putting the net into the boat

[11]   *múñ ísĭbáák íkèm*
        when the flow tide is just right

[12]   *mè ìrè ísĭtá íkèm*
        or the ebb tide is just right

[18]   *ísĭtàp njĭn ísáñá*
        when (you) finish putting the net

[22]   *ènyì ísĭré ókwááñ*
        when you (pl) reach the sea

[23]   *mè ènyì ísĭmúñ ŕîñ*
        and when you see fish

[26]   *ènyì ísĭtó ńjìn ísáñá*
        when you finish casting the net

[27]   *ńjìn yà ísĭkúp íñíñ*
        when the net stays long

[30]   *ènyì ísĭfó ŕé úwù kìnyì*
        when you (pl) arrive back at your house

Coda

[36–37]   *mônwọ̀n íbé*
            It will be good that

[38]   *áyá gwúñ ònû ìnyọ̀ñ*
        young child who comes into the world

[39–40]   *íkwééñ úbọ́k ékísí m̀bọ́m*
            to learn how to go fishing

Clearly, (209) does not represent the gist of the speaker's essential communicative goal, but (210) does. All the steps in (210) represent the description of the type of fishing which the speaker intends to present.

(210) Body

    [7]   ènyì mêdàsí ísí
           you (pl) will first go

    [8]   ítàp ńjìn mé újí mé átásùk
           to put the net in the boat at the riverside

    [10]   ènyì mêfò úwù
           you (pl) will go back to the house

    [13]   ènyì mê!nênŭtééñ úràñ
           you (pl) will then take paddles

    [14]   mè ímònó éwòp mè ágòk
           and take a scoop and (some) chewing sticks

    [15]   ítàp mé èmèn ókwùn
           (and) put (them) into a basket

    [16]   mè íbén ísìbí átásùk
           and carry it out to the river side

    [17]   ísí ítàp mé èmèn újí
           (and) put it in the boat

    [19–21]   ènyì mê!bêbènè íkíkóp ísìbí íkíníñ ókwááñ
           you (pl) will then begin to paddle out into the sea

    [24–25]   ènyì mê!bêbènè íkító ńjìn
           you (pl) will then begin to cast the net

    [28]   ènyì mê!nênŭtàbá ńjìn yà
           you (pl) will then begin to pull in the net

    [29]   mè íkíwáká íríñ
           and removing the fish

    [31]   ògwú ǹté újí mô!nênŭmònó íríñ
           the fishing boat owner will then take some fish

[32–33] ínyí ésâ étêm ùsùñ
(and) give for cooking stew

[34] mè ínyám èchí òsîsìk
and sell the rest

8.4 Tense and aspect in procedural grounding

The use of the different types of aspect in all the texts is summarized in (211). Since sequentiality is a crucial foreground element in procedural discourse, the best way to study this chart is to look at the uses of typically sequential versus nonsequential aspectual categories. Typically, the inchoative, inceptive, and perfective are sequential, while the imperfective (here continuous, habitual) and states are nonsequential. All the others may go either way. The discussion that follows proceeds from the perfective, inchoative, inceptive, and imperfective to states.

(211) Use of aspect in FISH, DANCE, FISH2, and CANON

	Phasal				Perfectivity			Inherent		
	INCH	INC	CMPL	IMM	PFTV	CONT	HAB	STA	ACT	ACC	ACH
FG	13	3	0	0	94	3	0	0	56	19	26
BG	2	0	12	9	127	5	15	52	42	21	31
Total	15	3	12	9	221	8	15	52	98	40	57

There are a total of 221 perfective verb forms in the four texts combined. Out of this, 127 (57%) occur in background materials while only 94 (43%) occur in foreground materials. The break-down of this number into foreground/background for each text is as follows: FISH 20/27, DANCE 15/15, FISH2 16/7, and CANON 43/78. These figures seem, erroneously, to indicate that the perfective is not a good indicator of the foreground. The truth is that compared with the imperfective, the perfective correlates quite highly with the foreground. Only 3 (12.5%) out of the 23 occurrences of the imperfectives are found in the foreground, while 94 (about 43%) out of the 221 occurrences of the perfectives occur in the foreground. Also, all occurrences of Dstem perfectives (which are optional here) are found in the foreground. The reasons for the apparent preponderance of the perfective in the background are as follows. First, in these texts there are many background explanations which are expressed with perfective verbs in subordinate conditional clauses. For instance, in CANON which has the largest number of background perfectives, as shown in the breakdown, the speaker gives a long discourse to describe what will happen to the cannon if it is placed wrongly or on soft ground. Secondly, the introductions and conclusions, which are all background material, contain many perfective verbs.

Another typical sequential aspect is the inchoative. In all the texts combined, there are 15 inchoative verbs and only 2 (13%) of them occur in the background. These are found in subordinate clauses in the first two paragraphs of the FISH text given in (202) and (203), the two paragraphs describing what equipment is necessary to qualify as a fisherman. These two subordinate clauses are also special in that they describe prerequisite steps. They do not just reiterate the previous steps. In this way, they encode sequentiality, and thus qualify to be classified as bonafide steps in the procedure. On the basis of these statistics, the function of the inchoative aspect in these texts is a good indicator of foreground in this genre.

The inceptive and the imperfective (continuous) are discussed together because all the occurrences of continuous aspect that express foreground events collocate with the inceptive. All three inceptives in the texts, marked by *bene* 'begin', two in FISH and one in DANCE, express foreground events. They express the inception of processes, and the processes are expressed with the continuous aspect to indicate their processual nature. It is not the entire process that is foregrounded, only its inception, as shown in (212) from FISH. Casting the net is a process, but its inception is foregrounded.

(212) ènyì **mê-!bê-bènè**   í-kí-tó   ńjĩn
      2pl cpl^FUT-REDUP-begin NSP-IMPF-cast net
      you will then begin to cast (the) net

It is only in this way that continuous events come to be mentioned in the foreground. The remaining 5 (66%) out of the total of 8 occurrences of the continuous aspect are used to express background events which overlap or are simultaneous with foreground events. This is the normal use of the continuous aspect.

Apart from the continuous, the other imperfective aspect exemplified in the texts is the habitual aspect. As expected, all 15 (100%) occurrences of the habitual aspect are found in background material. They are non-sequential, and therefore only occur in the background in discourse genres in which sequentiality is crucial, as it is in the procedural genre.

The stative verbs have no internal structure and do not involve a change of state. Therefore, they are nonsequential. In these texts, all 52 (100%) stative verbs occur in the background.

Among the other aspectual categories, the completive and immediacy consistently occur in background materials. All occurrences of them, 12

(100%) of completive and 9 (100%) of immediacy, are found in recapitulative subordinate consequential clauses. The other aspects, i.e., activities, accomplishments, and achievements, occur both in foreground and background materials.

Thus, all three types of aspect—perfectivity, inherent, and phasal—contribute to the foreground and background in the procedural discourse in Obolo. Diagnostically, the procedural foreground consists of the inchoative, inceptive (both phasal), and Dstem perfective (perfectivity) verbs, while the procedural background consists of the imperfective (perfectivity), completive and immediacy (both phasal), and stative (inherent) verbs.

The most distinctive difference between the two types of procedural discourse, i.e., those with projection and those without projection is in the tense. While both have nonfuture tense in their background, the foreground of procedurals with projection contains the future tense while that of procedurals without projection contains nonfuture tense. The exception to the rule of nonfuture background is the set of materials that occur in the "what-to-have" paragraphs which are background materials, yet expressed in the future. These paragraphs can be seen as quasi-procedures to the extent that having the prerequisite tools can well be taken as steps in the procedure. However, a piece of evidence to the contrary is seen in the CANON text. In this text, after describing "what-to-have," the next set of steps are introduced with the statement given in (213)

(213) òkpá-ótú ḿkpọ́ ó-bô-rọ̀ ì-rè
first thing 2sg-INT-do 3sg-be
The first thing to do is:

This statement clearly rules out the quasi-procedural steps as procedural steps, although they are expressed in the future. "What-to-have" paragraphs, which always precede the procedural steps ("what-to-do"), are all expressed in the future (except in FISH2), though they are background materials. Because of this, I refer to them as special procedural background. In the FISH text, the consequential clauses in these instances contain the *ni* inchoative verbs which are the leading sequential markers.

As a general summary to this section, the foreground of the procedural discourse with projection is defined as consisting of the future, inchoative, inceptive, with or without Dstem perfective verbs, while that of the projectionless procedural consists of all of the above with nonfuture instead of the future tense. The procedural background, for both types, is defined as consisting of nonfuture, imperfective, and stative verbs.

A summary of tense and aspect in procedural discourse from the most foregrounded to the most backgrounded is given in chart form in (214).

(214) Properties of foreground and background in FISH, DANCE, FISH2, and CANON texts

	Tense[45]	Key Aspect	Form	Other properties
FG	future	special PFTV	Dstem	sequential, main, (2/3 pers subj)[46]
	or	PFTV special INCH	*neni*	sequential, main/ coordinate
	nonfuture	PFTV INCH	*ni*	sequential, main
		PFTV INCH	*béné*	sequential, main
		other PFTV	∅	sequential, main/ coordinate/paratactic
		IMPF INC	*béné kí*	nonsequential, main
		other PFTV	∅	sequential, hypotactic, relative clause
		IMM	REDUP	sequential, hypotactic
		CMPL	*sáñá*	sequential, hypotactic
	other	IMPF	*ki*	nonsequential, any clause
BG	nonfuture	states	∅	nonsequential, any clause

---

[45]In the most foregrounded material, tense is future for procedural with projection and nonfuture for procedural without projection. In the most backgrounded material, it is nonfuture for both types of procedural.

[46]In the most foregrounded material, the subject of the main clause is usually 2nd person for procedural with projection and 3rd person for procedural without projection.

9
Tense and Aspect in Expository Discourse

The purpose of expository discourse is to explain something. In order to do this, it is necessary for the speaker to tell what the concept is, how it works, its function, and other relevant details. Expository discourse, according to Longacre (1985), is theme-oriented rather than agent-oriented.

Of the four texts in my database, the expository texts are the most abundant, and also the most heterogenous. Expository paragraphs are found embedded in the setting and background in narrative texts, in the introduction and conclusion in procedural texts, and also in the illustrations in hortatory texts. By itself, not embedded in any other genre, the expository discourse has other genres embedded in it. The two texts on which this chapter is based contain embedded procedural and contrast paragraphs which are discussed separately in chapters 8 and 10, respectively.

9.1 The data

The corpus of data for this study is made up of two expository texts, FISH2, an oral text spoken by a thirty-four-year-old man, and School Children (SC), a text written by a teenage boy about fifteen years old. This text is taken from a young people's magazine called *Ida Obolo eyi Nsabon* which means 'voice of Obolo for young people'.

FISH2 describes some aspects of fishing in general, mentioning differences in seasons, dry and rainy seasons, types of fish, and how to catch them. The manner of catching them includes some procedures, i.e., how to make certain of the nets and traps, and how to use them.

The SC text presents a description of school children in general from the author's perspective. He writes about their attitude towards their parents, morning and after school chores at home on school days, how the children differ from those who do not go to school, and what benefits they derive from education.

9.2 The structure

The two texts are similar in that they are not time bound; they describe situations that are true all the time or that recur seasonally. Therefore, the dominant temporal structure consists of habituality and the generic morpheme *rà* in the foreground. Besides being generic, both texts contain some procedural paragraphs, with and without projection, i.e., a situation or action which is contemplated or anticipated but not realized. Since the purpose of expository discourse is not to tell a story or prescribe the steps of an activity but rather to explain something, speakers often need to tell how things are put together and how they work. Thus, procedural paragraphs occur in these expository texts. The body of each of the texts contains a mixture of discourse types—explanatory, procedural, and contrast. Each type contributes to the exposition of the major topic discussed in the text.

General formulaic opening and closing statements, which are themselves expository, do not seem to be necessary. However, each text contains many subtopics, and the speakers go from one related subtopic to another. Each subtopic within the body of the text starts with a statement which introduces the topic. None of the texts has any general conclusion. One of them, the SC text, has an opening statement which introduces the topic and is elaborated all through the text. But the other, FISH2, does not have a separate opening statement. Rather, the topic, fishing, is introduced in a hypotactic clause at the beginning of the first paragraph of the text.

The opening statement. The SC text has an opening statement whereas FISH2 does not. In SC, the statement is a generic fact which the speaker believes to be true—school children are always wise, both at home and outside their homes. This statement is given in (215) where the main verb in the sentence is a nonfuture perfective stative verb *-re* 'to be'. The rest of the text is an explanation of the truth expressed by this statement.

(215) a. ǹsàbọ́n úwù-íkpá é-ré ǹsàbọ́n è-kî-rìọ̀ọ́ñ ínû
children school cpl-be children cpl-IMPF-know thing
School children are children who are knowledgable

b. í-béné mé úwù kìbàñ í-sà í-sìbí óyêt
NSP-begin PREP house 3pl^POSS NSP-take NSP-go^out outside
(in) their homes (and) outside.

The exposition. In this section, each text is discussed separately starting with school children (SC).

School Children (SC). The opening statement of SC is a summary statement and the rest of the text consists of subtopics that elaborate on it. The first subtopic is the attitude of school children towards their parents. Others are chores before school on school days, followed by after-school routines, and the benefits of being educated. Sandwiched in between chores before school and after-school routines is an unelaborated subtopic, a thesis that school children are habitually different from other children who do not go to school.

The attitude of school children towards their parents is expressed as a thesis followed by an elaboration. This, as well as some chores before school, the comparison with nonschool children, and one of the benefits, are discussed below for illustration. In terms of tense and aspect, nonfuture habitual statives and activities are used for the attitude and comparison sections, tense-neutral generic perfective activity for chores, and future perfective statives and activities for the benefit section. The genericness of the chores section is expressed by the morpheme *rà* on the first verb in the clause chain, followed by unneutralized pronominal prefixes on subsequent verbs after each overt conjunction in the chain.

(216) Attitude to parents

a. ǹsàbọ́n úwù-íkpá é-kí-lìbí ǹgá kìbàñ mèlék
children school cpl-IMPF-respect mother 3pl^POSS CONJ

ǹté kìbàñ
father 3pl^POSS
School children habitually respect their mothers and their fathers.

b. í-riá èmâ íkwààñ géèlék
3pl-send 3pl message any
(If) they send them on any errand

    c. *èmâ é-kí-sí-sî*
       3pl cpl-IMPF-REDUP-go
       they always go.

(217) Chores before school

    a. *úsèn géèlék ò-rê-rè   úsèn é-kí-sí   úwù-íkpá*
       day every 3sg-REDUP-be day cpl-IMPF-go school
       (On) any day in which people go to school (i.e., on every school day)

    b. *èmâ mî-rà í-nàñá í-kéké mé íláák mé àtá m̀gbọ̀*
       3pl cpl-GEN NSP-depart NSP-stand PREP sleep PREP good time
       they would wake up early

    c. *mè è-sî múdìm*
       CONJ cpl-go water
       and would go to fetch water

    d. *mè è-chân ìjọ̀ñ*
       CONJ cpl-sweep floor
       and would sweep the floor

(218) Comparison with nonschool children

ǹsàbọ́n úwù-íkpá é-kí-jé èsêsé mé lék èbí
children school cpl-IMPF-go different PREP body DET^pl

    é-kà-sî-gè úwù-íkpá
    cpl-NEG-go-REL school

School children are habitually different from those who do not go to school.

(219) Benefits

    a. *m̀gbọ̀ géèlék ó-sì-bé úwù-íkpá*
       time every 2sg-go-REL school
       When you are educated

    b. *òwù mô-riọ̀ọ̀ñ ísí èbí énê í-wá mé èsêsé*
       2sg 2sg^FUT-know face DET^pl people NSP-many PREP different

ámà
towns
you will know many people in different towns

c. mè í-rọ́ àtá ínû mé èmèn ámà òbòlò
   CONJ NSP-do good thing PREP inside town Obolo
   and (will) do good things in Obolo land.

d. mé m̀gbò yà ówùwà énê mê-riọ̀ọ̀ñ òwù ísí
   PREP time DDEM^sg many people cpl^FUT-know 2sg face
   At that time many people will know you

e. mè í-riọ̀ọ́ñ ámà kwùñ mè ídó kwùñ
   CONJ NSP-know town 2sg^POSS CONJ nation 2sg
   and (will) know your town and your nation.

Fishing 2 (FISH2). In FISH2, the opening statement is part of an extended paragraph that prepares the way for the rest of the text. This paragraph describes the change in the season that makes it favorable for fishing. The onset of the harmattan[47] is not a good time for fish. But when the harmattan blows for a long time, fish get used to its cold nights and hot days and begin to swim against this offshore wind into the rivers and creeks. Then it is time for the fishermen to do their work. In response to this abundance of fish, the rest of the text describes how the fishermen fish, what kinds of equipment they use, and how to make and use them.

The opening paragraph and a typical exposition about one of the fish, crayfish, are given below as an illustration of the text. The opening paragraph is given in (220)–(222), while the exposition on crayfish is given in (223)–(226). In terms of tense and aspect, these are mostly nonfuture habitual nonstatives. In (221) and (226), the aspectual combinations are sequential perfective nonstatives, while (221) is nonfuture, and (226) is tense-neutral. The habitual marker *kí* is reduplicated to *kékí* to emphasize the unending recurrence of the habitual situation in (220) and (222). The high tone pattern on this reduplication sets it apart from the !kêkî in narratives, which carries a distinctive fall from stepped high to low followed by a rise. Example (221) also contains durativity by repetition of the verb.

(220) a. mé ágàñ èyí èbí m̀bọ́m íríñ
        PREP side GENT^sg DET^pl occupation fish
        As for the fishermen's business

---

[47]Harmattan is the name of the cool dry North East Trade Wind that blows southwards from the Sahara desert. It gets to Obolo land on the coast in November each year and continues until late February.

b. *mé m̀gbọ̀ úrá ékìrìkà í-sǐ-bô-nù*
PREP time sun harmattan 3SG-CNS-INT-come
whenever the harmattan is about to come

c. *ókwááñ ì-ké-kí-fiéék*
sea 3SG-REDUP-IMPF-bad
the sea is (usually) bad (for fishing).

(221) a. *ékìrìkà í-sǐ-wùt í-wùt í-wùt í-wùt í-wùt*
harmattan 3SG-CNS-blow NSP-blow NSP-blow NSP-blow NSP-blow
When the harmattan blows and blows for a long time

b. *mè í-ní-bọ̀kọ́ ìrèk mé èmèn múñ*
CONJ NSP-INCH-receive position PREP inside water
and its effect is felt in the water,

c. *òtútúùk lék írîñ í-sǐ-bọ̀kọ́ útọ̀ọ̀k èyí ékìrìkà*
all body fish 3PL-CNS-receive cold GENT^sg harmattan
when the bodies of the fish get used to the cold of the harmattan

d. *mè ì-yáká í-ré úyòk èyí m̀gbọ̀ ékìrìkà sǐ*
CONJ 3SG-turn NSP-be heat GENT^sg time harmattan also
or the heat of the harmattan season also,

(222) a. *írîñ ì-ké-kí-níñ í-wá mé èmèn ókwááñ*
fish 3SG-REDUP-IMPF-enter NSP-many PREP inside big^river
many fish do habitually enter into the big rivers

b. *í-nàñá mé lék úbọ̀k*
3SG-arise PREP body manner
because of how

c. *éfét ó-kí-sà í-wùt éfét ìnyọ̀ñ*
wind 3SG-IMPF-take NSP-blow wind north
the wind blows, the north (east trade) winds.

d. *írîñ î-kì-nwáñá í-níñ mé ìbòt òkólò*
fish 3SG-IMPF-go^against^wind NSP-enter PREP upper^side creek

ò-kûp èsêsé èsêsé
3SG-stay different different
Fish habitually go against the wind into the upper parts of many different creeks

(223) a. írîn̄ é-kí-tét i-wá mé m̀gbò̩ úrá
fish CPL-IMPF-catch NSP-plenty PREP time sun
The fish which is usually caught plentifully during the dry season

b. ì-kí-ré ìko̩t
3SG-IMPF-be shrimp
is shrimp

c. èjì é-kí-gwén m̀fíríyàk mè ì-yáká í-ré ásákábàrí
1SG CPL-IMPF-call mfiriyak CONJ 3SG-turn NSP-be asakabari
(which) we call mfiriyak or asakabari.

(224) a. íko̩t èyí kèyâ é-kí-sí mé èmèn ókwáán̄ ílé
shrimp GENT^SG DDEM^SG CPL-IMPF-go PREP inside river great
That type of shrimp, (people) go for it in the great river

b. ò-rê-rè èmèn-àwàjì
3SG-REDUP-be ocean
which is the ocean.

(225) a. í-sĭ-sí í-sà ńjìn é-kí-gwén ǹkòtò í-sà í-tó
3PL-CNS-go NSP-take net CPL-IMPF-call nkoto NSP-take NSP-cast
Whenever they would go (and) cast the net called nkoto

b. mî-rà í-tét íko̩t yà
CPL-GEN NSP-catch shrimp DDEM^SG
they would catch that shrimp.

(226) é-ké-kí-tét i-wá mé m̀gbò̩ úrá í-gàk m̀gbò̩ ìbòt
CPL-REDUP-IMPF-catch NSP-plenty PREP time sun NSP-pass time rain
They always catch more of it during the dry season than during the rainy season.

9.3 Grounding in expository discourse

The discussions in this section and the next one do not include the procedural paragraphs embedded within the texts since procedural discourse has been discussed separately. Based on the principle of nuclearity adopted here for the isolation of foreground and background materials, the differences between foreground and background are observed in the distribution of clause types. Foreground material is found to consist mostly of main clauses while background materials are found to consist mostly of hypotactic and relative clauses. In the nonprocedural section of the texts, 96% of all the main clauses occur in the foreground; 91% of all the hypotactic clauses and 100% of all the relative clauses occur in the background. Both coordinate and complement clauses can go either way. These facts are illustrated in (227).

(227) Foreground and background clauses in SC and FISH2

	main		coordinate		hypotactic		complement		relative	
	no.	%	no.	%	no.	%	no.	%	no.	%
FG	24	96	7	50	1	9	16	50	0	0
BG	1	4	7	50	10	91	16	50	15	100
Total	25	100	14	100	11	100	32	100	15	100

Taking the SC text as an example, the foreground consists of what school children do, their attitudes to their parents, how they differ from nonschool children, and what benefits they get as a result of their going to school. The background consists of the descriptions of the contexts, situations, and conditions under which the foreground material is situated. The foreground and background of this text are exemplified below—background in (228), and foreground in (229). The numbers in square brackets refer to the number of each clause in the text.

(228) [3] *íbéné mé úwù kìbàñ ísà ísíbí óyêt*
from their homes outside

[5] *íriá èmâ íkwááñ gèèlék*
if the (parents) send them on any errands

[7] *úsèn gèèlék òrêrè úsèn*
(on) every day that is a day

[8] *ékísí úwù-íkpá*
(in which people) go to school

[18] *mé lék èbí ékàsîgè úwù-íkpá*
from those who do not go to school.

[31] *m̀gbọ̀ gèèlék ósìbé úwù-íkpá*
when you are educated

(229) [1] ǹsàbǫ́n úwù-úkpá éré ǹsàbǫ́n
School children are children

[2] èkîriǫ̀ǫ́ñ ínû
(who) are wise.

[4] ǹsàbǫ́n úwù-íkpá ékílìbí ǹgá kìbàñ mèlék ǹté kìbàñ
School children habitually respect their mothers and their fathers.

[6] èmâ ékísísî
They (never fail to go) on errands.

[9] èmâ mûrà ínàñá íkéké mé íláák mé àtá m̀gbǫ̀
They would wake early from sleep

[10] mè èsî múdĩm
and would go (to fetch) water,

[11] mè èchân ìjòñ
and would sweep the floor

[12] mè ètákà ágòk
and would chew the chewing stick

[13] mè ètǫ̀p èbí úwù kìbàñ ámòn
and would greet the people in their homes

[14] săbùm èmâ mênísí
before they would go

[15] íkén múñ
(and) bathe

[16] mè éjè úwù-íkpá
and would go off to school.

[17] ǹsàbǫ́n úwù-íkpá ékíjé èsêsé
School children appear (and behave) differently.

[32] òwù môriǫ̀ǫ̀ñ ísí èbí énê íwá mé èsêsé ámà
You will know many people in different towns,

[33] mè írọ́ àtá ínû mé èmèn ámà òbòlò
and do good things in Obolo towns.

[34] mé m̀gbọ̀ yà ówùwà énê mêriọ̀ọ̀ñ òwù ísí
At that time, many people will know you

[35] mè íriọ̀ọñ ámà kwùñ mè ídó kwùñ
and know your town and your nation.

A comparison of these two examples immediately reveals that (228) by itself does not contain the essential gist of what the author is trying to communicate, whereas (229), taken by itself, does. In (229), the author expresses all the facts that, in his view, make school children wise. In (228), the contexts and situations in which these essential facts are carried out are expressed. Therefore, (229) contains nuclear information while (228) contains supportive satellite information.

9.4 Tense and aspect in expository grounding

Expository discourse in Obolo tends to be tense-neutral. Since the expository genre is mainly explanatory, not chronological in nature, the foreground has aspectual categories that do not express sequentiality, while the background may contain both sequential and nonsequential aspectual categories. The aspects in the foreground include imperfectives, states, and any nonsequential phasal aspects, such as duratives and *yákà* inchoative. The *yákà* inchoative encodes contrasts rather than sequentiality although contrasts are not required in the genre.

The distribution of the three types of aspect in the two texts is given in (230) and the percentages of these figures in (231).

(230) Distribution of aspect in SC and FISH2

	Phasal				Perfectivity			Inherent			
	INCH	INC	CMPL	DUR	PFTV	CONT	HAB	STA	ACT	ACC	ACH
FG	3	0	0	0	29	6	13	13	22	0	13
BG	3	0	0	1	41	0	8	18	25	1	5
Total	6	0	0	1	70	6	21	31	47	1	18

(231) Distribution of aspect by percent

	Phasal				Perfectivity			Inherent			
	INCH	INC	CMPL	DUR	PFTV	CONT	HAB	STA	ACT	ACC	ACH
FG	50	0	0	0	41	100	62	42	47	0	72
BG	50	0	0	100	59	0	38	58	53	100	28

The tables in (230)–(231) reveal that the phasal aspects are not crucial in the structure of the expository discourse. This by itself distinguishes the expository from the other discourse types. The tables also reveal that, for perfectivity aspect, imperfective forms are used more commonly in the foreground of expository texts than in narrative and procedural. Almost 70% (19 out of 27) of all the imperfectives in the expository texts occur in the foreground as against 12.5% (3 out of 23) in procedural and 33.3% (2 out of 6) in the narrative texts. Secondly, for inherent aspect, only achievement is clearly an expository foreground aspect (13 out of 18 or 72%) while the others are more equally distributed. Thirdly, for phasal aspect, the inchoative is equally distributed instead of correlating with foreground as it did in both narrative and procedural. These tendencies are significant distinctive features of expository discourse.

We turn now to examine the aspectual character of the main, hypotactic and relative clauses which carry the diagnostic distinctions of expository foreground and background. The distribution of aspects in terms of sequentiality in is given in (232).

(232) Foreground and background in terms of sequentiality

		main	hypotactic	relative
FG:	nonsequential	18	1	0
	sequential	3	0	0
BG:	nonsequential	0	1	13
	sequential	1	7	2

Since sequentiality in relative clauses does not have any crucial effect on the character of grounding in discourse, the emphasis in this analysis is on main and hypotactic clauses. Of the twenty-one main clauses that occur in the foreground in these two texts, eighteen (86%) are nonsequential and three (14%) are sequential. The nonsequential clauses comprise six habitual activities, four habitual states, four perfective states, and one each of continuous state, continuous activity, continuous achievement, and habitual activity verbs. Of the eight hypotactic clauses in the background, seven (88%) are sequential while only one (12%) is nonsequential. Thus, the foreground of the expository discourse almost always consists of nonsequential aspects. Although sequentiality or nonsequentiality in relative clauses may not be very crucial, the presence of thirteen (87%) nonsequential and two (13%) sequential relative clauses in the background is significant enough to conclude that the background of expository discourse may consist of both sequential and nonsequential aspects.

With respect to tense, the general observation is that, regardless of grounding, expository discourse as a whole is neutral with respect to tense. Tense does not differ between foreground and background. Tense neutrality in the genre means that expositions may be given of any situation in the past, future, or even generically without regards to tense. This contrasts with narratives which often tend to be in the past. The two expository texts fall mainly in the generic category, although some parts were told in the future. The SC text contain a futuristic (or projected) set of benefits that accrue from education. But the condition for the benefits contains the generic temporal phrase m̀gbọ̀ gèèlék 'any/every time'. This defines a generic, all time, temporal context for the futuristic benefits which, when used in this way, encodes more the irrealis mode than future tense. The same applies to the future procedural paragraph embedded in the FISH2 text. This paragraph tells how to fish with a cast net. Because it is set in the generic, the temporal context of the entire text, the future tense marking here also encodes the irrealis mode rather than the future tense.

In summary, in terms of tense and aspect, the explanatory characteristic of the expository discourse calls for neutrality in tense. Even explanations of situations in the future, such as projected benefits, are couched in generic terms with respect to tense. This reduces the future-tense marking on the verbs in such paragraphs to irrealis marking. The same explanatory nature calls for a foreground that is nonsequential, marked by such aspectual categories as habitual, continuous, and states. There are a few foregrounded contrastive (also nonsequential) yákà inchoatives, in the contrast paragraphs. While the foreground of the expository discourse tends to consist of nonsequential aspectual categories, the background consists of both sequential and nonsequential aspects.

By virtue of the combination of these features identifying the foreground, the expository discourse genre subscribes to the cluster concept nature of the foreground. The table in (233) shows the arrangement of these components from the most foregrounded to the most backgrounded.

(233) Properties of foreground and background in SC and FISH2

	Tense	Key aspect	Form	Other properties
FG	tense-neutral	(IMPF) HAB	kí	nonsequential, main, coordinate
		(IMPF) CONT	kí	nonsequential, main, coordinate
		PFTV states	Ø	nonsequential, main, coordinate
		IMPF INCH	yáká	nonsequential, main, (contrastive)
BG		PFTV nonstates	Ø	sequential, hypotactic, complement, relative clauses

10
Tense and Aspect in Expository Compare-and-Contrast Discourse

Strictly speaking, the compare-and-contrast discourse is a subtype of the expository discourse, not a separate genre by itself. However, in Obolo, tense and aspect function in a unique way in the structure of the compare-and-contrast text, as compared to ordinary expository texts. Therefore, it is treated separately, rather than as a part of the expository discourse chapter.

Fries (1983) argues that Halliday's "theme" (Halliday 1967), realized by the initial elements in a sentence in English, has a direct correlate in the organization of the discourse. He shows that in a compare-and-contrast text, such as the Progress (PROGS) text, it is the successive themes which reveal that the text is organized in terms of comparing and contrasting.

10.1 The data

The PROGS text in my database is a written magazine article in which the author, a twenty-eight-year-old man, compares the state of affairs in Obolo today with what it used to be in the past, to show the progress from past times to today. The emphasis on time, past versus present, makes the PROGS text a time-based expository compare-and-contrast text. The comparison shows progress in five areas: housing, relation with the neighboring Okoloba people, religion, education, and language development. The discussion in each section is self-contained, and no attempt is made to connect it to the discussion in the adjacent section. There is no conclusion to the text.

10.2 The structure

Structurally, the text begins with an overall bipartite thesis followed by an introduction to the list of areas of comparison. Each area is discussed in two parts, first the past state of affairs, then the present state of affairs. Each of the parts begins with a main-line thesis or antithesis which is elaborated in the section. The thesis states the former state of affairs, and the antithesis, which states the present state of affairs, indicates that the previous state has come to an end and is replaced by a new and more favorable situation. To mark the contrast even more overtly, all the antitheses start with the contrastive conjunction *iré* 'but'. The progress is seen in the comparison. The picture illustrated here is that of the evil of the past being overcome by the good of the present. The schema of this text is presented in (234).

(234) Megathesis: Thesis 1
    Elaboration
  Thesis 2
    Elaboration
Mega-elaboration: Introduction
    List of areas:
    (1) Housing: Thesis
                    Elaboration
                  Antithesis
                    Elaboration
    (2) Okoloba: Thesis
                    Elaboration
                Antithesis
                  Elaboration
    (3) Religion: Thesis
                    Elaboration
                Antithesis
                  Elaboration
    (4) Education: Thesis
                    Elaboration
                Antithesis
                  Elaboration
    (5) Language: Thesis
                    Elaboration
                Antithesis
                  Elaboration

As (234) illustrates, there are two types of paragraph structures in the text: a megaparagraph which consists of both a thesis paragraph and an antithesis paragraph; and an ordinary paragraph, which consists of a thesis or antithesis and an elaboration. For instance, the Housing section is a megaparagraph, while the thesis section in it is an ordinary paragraph. The text begins with a bipartite megathesis for which the rest of the text is a mega-elaboration.

Since the past and present time references have no morphological marking, each section begins with a temporal phrase or a temporal adverbial: *(mé) m̀gbọ̀ òrâràkà* '(in) time past' for the past time part and *mé chérékyí* 'on this-day (i.e., today)' for the present time part. The temporal frame so established is assumed throughout the elaboration in the section. The sequence of these initial contrastive elements or themes indicate that the organization of the PROGS text is that of a compare-and-contrast text.

A typical megaparagraph is given in (235) to illustrate the structure. It consists of two ordinary paragraphs: a thesis paragraph from (a) to (f) and an antithesis paragraph from (g) to (l). The thesis is expressed in (a) to (c) and elaborated in (d) to (f), while the antithesis is expressed in (g) to (i) and elaborated in (j) to (l). The thematic elements discussed above are all bolded in the example.

(235) a. ***mé   m̀gbọ̀   ò-râ-ràkà***
PREP   time   3sg-REDUP-pass
In the past,

b. ***èbí   ǹté-ǹté   kìjì   kpè-kí-má***
DET^pl   forefather   1pl^POSS   cpl^NEG-IMPF-like
our forefathers did not like

c. *í-sâ-sà   àlàlá   í-chít   ìnyọ̀ñ   úwù   kìbàñ*
NSP-REDUP-take   zinc   NSP-cover   top   house   3pl^POSS
to roof their houses with roofing zinc.

d. ***òrộmùjọ̀ñ   kìbàñ   ì-jéêñ   í-bé***
tradition   3pl^POSS   3sg-teach   NSP-say
Their tradition taught

e. *ké   yộk-òbòlò   ì-ká-kì-sǎ   chiéèñ   ì-múñ   àlàlá*
COMP   god-Obolo   3sg-NEG-IMPF-take   eye   NSP-see   zinc
that the god of Obolo does not like to see roofing zinc

f. *ké   ì-kí-níñ   ọ́mộ   chiéèñ*
COMP   3sg-IMPF-enter   3sg   eye
that it dazzles him.

g. *íré mé chérékèyí yê*
   but PREP today   QUES
   But what about today?

h. *òjêlèk ínû   ò-kûp   ìkéyà*
   type thing 3sg-stay like^that
   that type of thing

i. *ì-kâ-yáká   ì-kúp*
   3sg-NEG-INCH NSP-stay
   is no more there.

j. *òwùwà énê   mé òwùwà ámà mé chérékèyí é-yáká*
   many people PREP many town PREP today   cpl-INCH

   í-kí-sà   àlàlá
   NSP-IMPF-take zinc
   Today, many people in many towns now use zinc

k. *í-tòóñ   mé   ìnyòñ úwù*
   NSP-place PREP top   house
   to roof (their) houses

l. *mégê í-ré   ókwááñ-m̀bọ́m*
   even NSP-reach fishing-port
   even up to the fishing port.

The organization of the PROGS text has a typical arrangement of thematic elements of a compare-and-contrast text where the thematic element occurs paragraph-initially, and is followed by the nonthematic elaboration. The themes in PROGS are doublets, a thesis and an antithesis, but the arrangement is the same. The entire text mirrors the structure of the ordinary paragraph, having a megathesis which is followed by a mega-elaboration that constitutes the rest of the text.

10.3 Grounding in compare-and-contrast discourse

The structure of the compare-and-contrast text consists of a series of theses or antitheses, each followed by an elaboration or explanation. The foreground consists of the assertions and counter assertions made in terms of theses and antitheses, respectively, while the background consists of the grounds for the assertions given in terms of elaborations or explanations. Using example (235) as an illustration, the thesis in (a) to

(c) and the antithesis in (g) to (i) constitute the foreground, while the elaborations in (d) to (f) and in (j) to (l) constitute the background.

10.4 Tense and aspect in grounding in compare-and-contrast discourse

Unlike the general expository genre, in which the preferred time reference is the tense-neutral generic (see chapter 9), the PROGS text is written in the nonfuture time frame. Since the comparison in this text is time-based, and time expression is therefore obligatory, temporal phrases are used to distinguish between the past and the present because the past/present distinction is not marked morphologically in the language.

In terms of aspect, the unique property that sets the compare-and-contrast text apart from an ordinary expository text is the presence of the *yákà* inchoative in the compare-and-contrast text. The difference between the two inchoative morphemes, *ni* and *yákà*, is that while *ni* occurs in sequential contexts, e.g., narrative and procedural discourse, *yákà* occurs in nonsequential contexts. Like its *ni* counterpart, *yákà* indicates that the event in question was not there before, that is, that there has been a change in the state of affairs. Therefore, it is only fitting that it occurs in the antitheses, not in the theses. The *yákà* inchoative does not occur in any of the theses, but it occurs with the contrastive conjunction, *ìré* 'but' in three of the five antitheses. The *yákà* inchoative is not necessary in the ordinary expository discourse.

As in ordinary expository texts, the foreground materials in the PROGS text are uniformly nonsequential, while the background materials are a mixture of sequential and nonsequential materials. Specifically, all the theses, including the bipartite megathesis at the beginning of the text, and the contrastive antitheses (foreground material), are expressed in aspectual combinations involving the imperfective or stative aspects or both, while the elaborations (background material) are expressed in both imperfective and stative combinations as well as perfective nonstative combinations. This fact is illustrated in (236) and exemplified in (237).

(236) Sequentiality in compare-and-contrast text

	Nonsequential	Sequential
FG	22	0
BG	42	45

In (237a), the thesis, the verb *òkíbóló* 'is waking up' is a present progressive achievement, and in (237b), the elaboration of the thesis, the verb *ínùñ* '(has) entered' is a nonfuture perfective achievement.

(237) a. mé   àtíkộ   òbòlò   ò-kí-bóló
       PREP   truth   Obolo   3sg-IMPF-wake^up (PROG ACH)
       truly Obolo is waking up

   b. míjè   ówùwà   ùnwèné   î-nùñ   mé   èmèn   òbòlò   mé
       because many   changes 3sg-enter PREP inside Obolo   PREP

      chérékèyí   í-gàk   iyâkwùt   ò-râ-ràkà
      today   NSP-pass   adjacent^day 3sg-REDUP-pass
      because many changes (have) entered Obolo (PFTV ACH) today
      than yesterday

A typical thesis/antithesis opposition without the elaborations is illustrated in (238). In the thesis, (238a), the verb ìkíkpộ...ísìkí 'look down' is past, habitual, stative; and in the antithesis, (238b), the verb éyáká íré 'they (now) are' is a present, perfective, inchoative, state.

(238) a. m̀gbộ   ò-râ-ràkà   ògwú   ínyâ   ì-kí-kpộ   ògwú
         time   3sg-REDUP-pass   DET^sg Okoloba 3sg-IMPF-look   DET^sg

         òbòlò   chiééñ   í-sìkí   ènénén
         Obolo   eye   NSP-low   very^much
         In the past, the Okoloba people (habitually) looked down on
         Obolo people very much.

   b. íré   mé   chérékèyí   yê   èbí   òbòlò   é-yáká   í-ré   èbí
      but   PREP   today   QUES DET^pl   Obolo   cpl-INC   NSP-be DET^pl

      íbòt   mé   ótú-ágộộk   m̀kpùlú   èyí   kìbàñ
      head   PREP   branch   government   GEN^sg   3pl^POSS
      But what about today? Obolo people are now rulers in their
      own branch of the government

The two parts of the megathesis consist of a present, progressive, achievement situation and a present, perfective, inchoative, stative situation. Further, in all of the five sections in the list, the theses consist uniformly of past, habitual, stative situations, but the antitheses are not so homogeneous. Of the five antitheses, three consist of present, perfective, inchoative, stative situations, while the remaining two consist of a present, progressive, achievement situation and a present, perfective, stative situation.

In summary, the time-based compare-and-contrast text differs from the ordinary expository discourse in its emphasis on time reference and the presence of the yáká inchoative, two properties that are not necessary in the ordinary expository discourse. Apart from these, the compare-and-contrast text shares the crucial property of nonsequentiality of the foreground with ordinary expository texts. In the expository texts generally, the background may be either sequential or nonsequential.

As in chapter 9, the compare-and-contrast expository discourse conforms to the cluster concept nature of the foreground. The foreground/background continuum is shown in (239), with the properties arranged from the most foregrounded to the most backgrounded. In place of tense-neutrality in the ordinary expository discourse, the time-based compare-and-contrast expository has past versus present time references. Also, the contrastive imperfective states and imperfective non state clauses are higher in salience in the compare-and-contrast discourse than in the ordinary expository discourse.

(239) Properties of foreground and background in PROGS text

	Tense	Key aspect	Form	Other properties
FG	past/today	(IMPF) HAB	kí	nonsequential, main, coordinate
		(IMPF) cont	kí	nonsequential, main, coordinate
		IMPF INCH states	yáká	nonsequential, main, (contrastive)
		IMPF INCH nonstates	yáká	nonseqential, main, (contrastive)
		PFTV states	∅	nonsequential, main, coordinate
BG		PFTV nonstates	∅	sequential, hypotactic, complement, relative clause

The PROGS text consists of a megathesis and a mega-elaboration which comprise five sections. Each section consists of a megaparagraph which consists of a thesis paragraph and an antithesis paragraph. Each paragraph consists of a main claim, thesis or antithesis, and an elaboration. The theses and antitheses comprise the foreground, while the elaborations comprise the background. The predominance of the imperfective and stative situations in the theses and antitheses (i.e., foreground) depicts the nature of the PROGS text as basically an expository text that describes the state of affairs. In the same way, the occurrence of inchoative states in the antitheses imply changes of situation or discontinuity of previous states of affairs. The background, as in all expository texts, consists of both sequential and nonsequential material.

11
Tense and Aspect in Hortatory Discourse

Hortatory discourse is one kind of "behavioral discourse" because it is meant to have an effect on human behavior. Its purpose is to modify the conduct of the receivers of the text. In such discourse there is a line of exhortation carried by imperative or modal forms which command, suggest, or urge some action, and everything else supplements or supports this line of exhortation.[48] In Obolo, sequentiality (expressed by aspect) is not crucial in the hortatory discourse genre which means that the exhortations may be given with or without sequentiality. Furthermore, the foreground remains either tense-neutral or is expressed in the future tense.

11.1 The data

The database for this chapter consists of two different types of hortatory texts—an oral indirect advice text (ADV) and a written type of warning (WARN), given by two adult males, both of whom are about thirty-four years of age.[49] In the first, ADV, the speaker tells the advice he would give to a

---

[48]See Longacre 1983 and 1992.
[49]Basic or minimal hortatory discourses also exist in the language, where someone in authority gives an order to a minor. These are usually unmitigated commands given with imperatives, and usually short, only a few clauses in length. Since Warning contains exhortation that is very similar to this kind of command, I do not discuss such minimal hortatory texts here.

young person who refuses to go to school. In the second, which is taken from the *Ida Obolo* magazine (Vol. 4, 1992), the author is addressing a very sensitive issue, an inter-family feud which resulted in the burning down of many houses in the town. This sensitivity is reflected in the degree of caution that he takes as he presents the issue. He uses a lot of expository illustrations, and compares and contrasts the people concerned (referred to generically) with the characters in the illustrations. He points out the problem indirectly, evaluates it, makes a mild accusation, and finally zeroes in on some groups of individuals who could possibly solve the problem, and calls on them directly to do something about the problem. But in urging them, he cautiously encodes his exhortations by means of negative imperatives. This text starts out as a beautiful satire, but gradually becomes nonsatirical, as far as it can politely go.

11.2 The structure

Although the structure of each of these texts is slightly different, pragmatically reflecting the social nature of the issues involved, the two texts contain the same types of components. Both texts contain an expression of the problem, some sort of motivation, and an exhortation. These components come in different positions in each of the two texts, as shown in (240). While ADV has exhortation at the beginning and at the end, WARN has the major exhortation at the end, and repeats a formulaic type of exhortations at the end of each illustration, making the text poetic-like. In both texts the problem and the major exhortation occur together in the same unit which is the first unit for ADV and the last unit for WARN, but not in the middle unit for either one. In both texts, the exhortation occurs in more than one unit, in the first and last units in ADV, and in all three units in WARN. Each text has three major natural divisions referred to in (240) as units. The components of the units are dissimilar.

(240) Stucture of ADV and WARN

	ADV		WARN
Unit 1	Problem	Unit 1	Illustration 1
	Exhortation		Comparison
Unit 2	Motivation		Formulaic exhortation
Unit 3	Exhortation	Unit 2	Illustration 2
			Illustration 3
			Comparison
			Formulaic exhortation

Unit 3 Comparison
        Problem
        Evaluation
        Main exhortation
        Formulaic exhortation

The structure of each text is discussed separately since there is no structural uniformity between them. The discussion begins with ADV, the simpler text.

ADV, **Unit 1.** This text begins with an expression of the problem followed immediately by the exhortation. These two components constitute the first unit. The problem itself, a young person refusing to go to school, is couched in an embedded relative clause. The exhortation is given in a complement clause, as indirect reported speech, since the speaker was not addressing the young person directly. Both components are given in (241). In terms of tense and aspect, the problem, in (241b), is expressed with a nonfuture perfective stative verb, while the exhortation, in (241d), is given in the tense-neutral hortative mood.

(241) a. *íré èmì ḿmúñ lék gwúñ*
      if 1sg 1sg-see body child
      If I see a young person

   b. *ògwú í-kà-chíéèk-gè   í-bô-sì   úwù-íkpá*
      DET^sg 3sg-NEG-agree-NEG^REL NSP-INT-go school
      who does not want to go to school

   c. *èmì mâ-tùmù   í-nyí   í-bé*
      1sg 1sg^FUT-speak NSP-give NSP-say
      I will say to him/her

   d. *ógwú í-sî   úwù-íkpá*
      DET^sg 3sg^HORT-go school
      let him/her go to school.

ADV, **Unit 2.** This unit consists of the motivation for the exhortation. The motivation is given in terms of benefits, which include economic benefit, good appearance, respect, boldness in traveling, and helpfulness to one's clan in various ways. Some of these are given in the future tense, while others are given in the nonfuture. Some are sequential, with perfective nonstatives, while others are nonsequential, with perfective states or imperfective states or non states. Example (242) illustrates the future nonstative motivation, while example (243) illustrates the nonfuture imperfective stative motivation.

(242) a. í-nàñá   mé   lék   òwù   ò-kpô-yákà   í-bọ̀kọ́   úfiâlèk
      NSP-arising PREP body 2sg 2sg-FUT^NET-INCH NSP-receive trouble

      òɡbògbò
      many
      because you will no more suffer too much

   b. săbùm   òwù   ò-yákà   ò-nò-riê
     before 2sg 2sg-ITER 2sg-INCH-eat
     before you eat.

(243) a. èbí   gèèlék   èbí   kpĕ-sí   íkpá
      DET^pl every DET^pl cpl^NEG-go book
      All the (people) who do not go to school

   b. kpè-kí-jààñ   mé   ònííñ
     cpl^NEG-IMPF-beautiful PREP road
     do not appear beautiful on the road.

The motivation section of the ADV text is formally closed with a conclusive statement that wraps up all the benefits. This summary statement is given in (244). Tense is nonfuture throughout, while aspectual combinations consist of perfective stative and habitual (imperfective) activity.

(244) éyí   ì-rè   íkwààñ   íkpá   ó-kí-sí
      PDEM^sg 3sg-be work book 3sg-IMPF-do
      This is the benefit of school (lit. what going to school achieves).

ADV, Unit 3. The third unit of the ADV text consists of a restatement of the exhortation which is given in unit 1, only here it is more like a suggestion than a command. The exhortation is given in (245b, c) with a nonfuture perfective stative verb and a future perfective activity verb, respectively.

(245) a. éyâ   ò-rọ́
      DDEM^sg 3sg-make
      Therefore

   b. î-nwọ́ñ   í-bé   gwúñ   gê mé lék
     3sg-good NSP-say child every
     it is good that every child

c. mô-sì   íkpá
3sg^FUT-go book
(should) go to school.

The exhortation which occurs both at the beginning and at the end of the text, could be argued to be points of rhetorical salience in a monologue. The problem also comes at the very beginning of the text. The entire middle section of the text is taken up by the motivation, which employs a combination of the nonfuture generic and future tense marking to indicate generic and anticipatory irrealis modes, respectively. The exhortations are both expressed in complement clauses, as indirect reported speech, because they are given indirectly. While the first one, being in the hortative mood, is neutral to tense, the second one is expressed as a suggestion in the future tense, because for a new-born child schooling is futuristic and anticipatory.

Warning. Like the ADV text, the WARN text also has three hortatory components which are also arranged in three major units. However, they are positioned differently from those in the ADV text. Rather than motivation which consists of benefits in the ADV text, the WARN text has illustrations, evaluations, and comparisons which help to warn against a particular type of behavior. Rather than indirect exhortations as in the ADV text, exhortations in the WARN text are direct and specific. There are two types of exhortations, first a formulaic one which occurs at the end of every unit and is addressed to Obolo as a nation. It is a direct call on the Obolo nation to look into the matter, and it is given in the affirmative without any threat. The second type is the main group of exhortations, all expressed in the negative to make them a little less direct. One of these, which is directed to the chiefs, comes with a mild accusation. The other two, directed to the educated elites and the young men and women of Obolo, come with a mitigated threat. This major exhortation comes in unit 3 at the end of the text, again a point of rhetorical salience. Unlike the ADV text where the problem occurred in unit one at the beginning of the text, the problem in the WARN text is placed in the last unit. The text gradually develops up to the point where the problem is unfolded, immediately followed by the major exhortations which provide a possible solution. The problem itself is given in two parts, the first followed by some comparison with previous illustrations, and the second by a condemnatory evaluation.

The text is discussed below, unit by unit. The first two units are similar: each starts with an illustration, which is followed by an evaluation, a comparison of the characters in the illustration with the troublemakers in Obolo, and finally a formulaic exhortation which calls on the Obolo nation to look into the matter. The only difference between the two is that the second unit contains two illustrations rather than one. The third unit is different from the first two in that it is the culmination of the first two units. It starts with comparisons and application of all the illustrations to the situation in Obolo. This is followed by the expression of the problem and the major exhortations consecutively. The unit closes with the same formulaic exhortation as do the first two units. Since unit 2 is similar to unit 1, only units 1 and 3 are discussed below.

WARN, Unit 1. This unit begins with an illustration about the cuttlefish. It tells about how the cuttlefish habitually leaves muddy waters for clear water. But when it meets a predator in the clear water, it shoots out its ink to reduce visibility and moves backwards, retreating back into the muddy water out of which it came. The illustration is an expository paragraph with tense-neutral generic nonsequential habitual actions. Following the illustration, the author immediately gives his own evaluation of it, and compares the cuttlefish, its ways and intentions, with troublesome human beings, their ways and their intentions. The evaluation, comparison, a typical questioning of man's motivation for evil, and the formulaic exhortation are given in (246)–(249), respectively. In terms of tense and aspect, the evaluation, comparison, and questions consist of a mixture of nonfuture and future, with sequential perfective nonstatives, and nonsequential perfective statives and imperfective nonstatives. The exhortation is in the hortative mood which is neutral to tense, but has sequential perfective nonstative aspectual combination.

(246) Evaluation
    a. *íjè   ò-kûp   ìkéyà*
       journey 3sg-stay like^that
       A journey like that

    b. *ì-kâ-kááñ   ñjè-ñnyĭ-ísí*
       3sg-NEG-have progress
       has no progress (*lit.* moving forward).

(247) Comparison
    a. *kúbǫ́k òfírìkòsók énê   ì-kí-nàñá   mé   èmèn   ùdûn*
       like cuttlefish person 3sg-IMPF-depart PREP inside darkness
       Like the cuttlefish, a person habitually departs from darkness

    b. *m̀gbǫ̀ í-kà-bólò-gè   chíèèñ*
       time 3sg-NEG-open-NEG^REL eye
       (where he is) when he is not wise/civilized

Tense and Aspect in Hortatory Discourse

    c. *í-nűñ   mé èmèn útòóñ*
       NSP-enter PREP inside light
       (to/and) enter(s) into light

    d. *m̀gbọ̀ î-bòlò-bé chíéèñ*
       time 3sg-open-REL eye
       when he has become wise/civilized.

    e. *ófírìkòsók ì-múñ ínû*
       cuttlefish 3sg-see thing
       The cuttlefish saw something

    f. *mô-sâk-bé ọ́mộ únán mé èmèn múñ ò-tô-tòòñ*
       3sg^FUT-injure-REL 3sg injury PREP inside water 3sg-REDUP-clear
       which would hurt it in the water which is clear.

    g. *ké î-bàálék í-tàp ùdŭn*
       COMPL 3sg-mention NSP-put darkness
       That is why it caused darkness

    h. *míjè kpùnû ònííñ géègè*
       because no way any
       because there is no other way

    i. *í-bô-sà í-nwọ̀nọ́*
       3sg-DFUT-take NSP-escape
       by which it would escape

    j. *í-lọ́ mé ìkéyà*
       NSP-miss PREP like^that
       apart from that.

(248) Question
    a. *ìrè kpàsî ònííñ ké énê ó-sà í-kááñ ùnén*
       QUES what^type way COMP person 3sg-take NSP-have right
       In what way does a person have the right

    b. *í-tâ-tàp ùdŭn mé èmèn útòóñ*
       NSP-REDUP-put darkness PREP inside light
       to cause darkness in the light?

(249) Formulaic exhortation
```
ídó      òbòlò   í-tâp             chíèèñ    í-kpộ
nation   Obolo   cpl^IMP-put       eye       cpl^IMP-look
```
Obolo nation, look into (it).

Thus, it can be seen that the first unit of the WARN text consists of an illustration about the cuttlefish, an evaluation of the illustration by the author, and a comparison of the cuttlefish and its characteristic behavior with troublesome human beings. The comparison involves the use of some rhetorical questions which help to express a negative judgment on the situation which the author is gradually unfolding. Right after the questions comes the formulaic exhortation. It is formulaic because the same sentence occurs at the end of every unit. In other words, the unit builds up from an expository illustration to negative evaluations, to questions, and finally to direct exhortation. The exhortation is given in the imperative mood, not indirectly by means of a hortative mood or a suggestive future tense indicative mood as in the ADV text. All tense is in the nonfuture, except a few anticipated situations which are expressed in the future.

WARN, Unit 3. This unit is very different from the first two. It is the culmination of all the other units. Rather than with illustrations, it begins with comparisons, questions, and evaluations, based on all the illustrations in units 1 and 2. The comparisons are immediately followed by the overt expression of the problem, which has not been mentioned up to this point. The expression of the problem is followed by a condemnatory and negative evaluation. After this come the major exhortations, directed at specific groups of people, in the imperative mood but expressed in the negative instead of the affirmative. The fact that this unit applies all the illustrations cumulatively from unit 1 and 2, and also contains both the problem and the major exhortations, sets it apart as unique.

The problem and the specific exhortations are given in (250)–(254). The problem is expressed in two parts, (250a) and (251a), both in subordinate clauses, in two consecutive sentences and in nonfuture imperfective nonstative aspectual combinations. The exhortations themselves, given in (252)–(254), are expressed by means of negative imperatives with a mixture of perfective nonstatives (sequential), and perfective statives and imperfective nonstatives (nonsequential) aspects.

(250) Problem
```
   a. èyí      énê      ó-kí-tàp          úkáñ   mé     lék    úwù    kàñ
      DET^sg   person   3sg-IMPF-put      fire   PREP   body   house  3sg^POSS
```
While man was setting fire on his house

b. ìrè   áyì   ò-rê-rè   èbí   íbọ́ọ́ñ
   QUES grandma 3sg-REDUP-be DET^pl chief
   was grandma, that is, the chiefs

c. èbí   mê-kọ̀t-bé   í-nèñé   énê   í-sùñ
   DET^pl cpl^FUT-be^able-REL NSP-arrange people NSP-keep

   kpùnû
   not^present
   who settle disputes among the people, not present?

(251) Problem
a. èyí   énê   ó-kí-gwàk   ámà
   DET^sg person 3sg-IMPF-tear town
   While man was tearing (down) the town

b. mé   èrìééñ èjì   é-nyé-nyê   lék   í-gó
   PREP name 1pl cpl-REDUP-strong body NSP-very^much
   in the name of "we are very strong,"

c. èjì é-wá-wâ   í-gó
   1pl cpl-REDUP-many NSP-very^much
   "we are very many,"

d. ìrè   tété   ò-rê-rè   kọ́nsìn   kpùnû
   QUEST grandpa 3sg-REDUP-be government not^present
   was grandpa, that is, the government, not present?

(252) Exhortation to the Chiefs
a. èbí   úbọ́ọ́ñ òbòlò í-kà-ríááñ   érè   ì-kì-kpọ̌
   DET^pl chiefs Obolo cpl^IMP-NEG-be^silent place NSP-IMPF-look
   Chiefs of Obolo, don't just look on in silence.

b. ùsíní chí   ì-nàñá   mé   íbòt kìnyì
   some PDEM^pl 3sg-depart PREP head 3pl^POSS
   Some of these (things) are (happening) because of you.

(253) Exhortation to the educated elites
a. èbí   íkpá   òbòlò í-kà-kéké
   DET^pl book Obolo cpl^IMP-NEG-stand
   Educated people of Obolo, don't just stand

b. mè ì-kát úbọ́k
   CONJ NSP-fold hand
   and fold your hands.

c. èsìp kàñ ì-kúp mé lék kìnyì
   shame 3sg^POSS 3sg-stay PREP body 3pl^POSS
   The shame (of these things) is on you.

(254) Exhortation to the young people
a. ǹsàbọ́n íríéèñ mè ǹsàbọ́n íbáàñ òbòlò í-kà-nwĕ
   children male CONJ children female Obolo cpl^IMP-NEG-open

   chíéèñ ì-kî-kpọ̌
   eye NSP-IMPF-look
   Young men and women of Obolo don't just open your eyes to look

b. mé é-kà-tâp-gè úbọ́k î-gòọ́k ì-rọ̌
   PREP cpl-NEG-put-NEG^REL hand NSP-follow NSP-do
   without giving a helping hand.

c. ùkwòòk kàñ ì-bô-kèmè ènyì
   burden 3sg^POSS 3sg-DFUT-press 2pl
   The burden of it is going to be on you.

As is the case with the other units, this unit comes to a close with the same formulaic exhortation, which is given in (255).

(255) ídó òbòlò ì-tâp chíéèñ ì-kpộ
      nation Obolo cpl^IMP-put eye cpl^IMP-look
      Obolo nation, look into (it).

11.3 Grounding in hortatory discourse

In line with his proposal that every monologue discourse has main-line events and supportive material, Longacre (1992:n6) points out that in hortatory discourse there is a line of exhortation carried by imperative or modal forms which command, suggest, or urge some action. Everything else in the hortatory text supplements or supports the line of exhortation. The line of exhortation forms the foreground while the support material forms the background in the hortatory genre.

The two texts in Obolo on which this chapter is based follow the same pattern. Without the exhortations, the motivation in the ADV text and the illustrations in the WARN text are simply expository texts which do not command, suggest, or urge any action on the part of the receiver of the texts. Therefore, they function as supportive material to the exhortations. Compared to these, the exhortation is minimal in size. In the WARN text for instance, out of the 130 clauses that make up the text, only 10 (8%) express exhortation. Of all the genres studied in this work, this unique characteristic where the foreground material consists of only 8% of the bulk of the text, only occurs in the hortatory genre. Thus, the basic hortatory text, that is, simple command, is the shortest of all discourse types.

Out of the 13 exhortation clauses in both texts, 10 are expressed in the imperative mood, and two in the hortative mood, which is related to the imperative (see chapter 2). Both moods are tense-neutral, i.e., they carry neither future nor nonfuture time reference. However, the remaining exhortation clause is expressed indirectly as a suggestion, in the indicative mood and in the future tense. Although this is only one out of 13 exhortations, it is my impression that this occurs quite often in the language. This one occurrence of a future indicative exhortation is given in (256).

(256) î-nwọ̀n   í-bé   gwúñ gê mé lék mô-sì   íkpá
      3sg-good NSP-say child every   3sg^FUT-go book
      It is good that every child...should go to school.

The presence of direct exhortation, expressed by unmitigated imperatives, indirect exhortations expressed by the hortative mood, and more indirect exhortations expressed by the indicative in combination with the future tense, suggests a scalar property in the foreground of the hortative discourse genre.

Apart from the exhortations which directly command and suggest actions in these texts, other structures also indirectly suggest and urge actions on the part of the receivers. These are found especially in the WARN text and they consist of the evaluations and comparisons. They suggest or urge proper behavior by condemning the improper behavior. They are expressed in the indicative mood in both future and nonfuture time reference. Although they somehow perform a similar function, they do not qualify as foreground material, but they are functionally different from the illustrations which do not urge any action. Therefore in this context, they are higher level background material. In this way, the background is seen to also possess a scalar property, as does the foreground. The background in this genre consists of other components of the hortatory schema, namely, motivation, problem, and authority whenever present.

11.4 Tense and aspect in hortatory grounding

The two texts in this study indicate that hortatory discourse does not distinguish between sequentiality and nonsequentiality, and tense may be future or neutral. The reason for this nondistinction between sequentiality and nonsequentiality is that exhortations may be expressed by imperfective (i.e., habitual and continuous) and stative verbs, as well as by perfective and nonstative verbs.

The distribution of tense and aspect in the two texts in terms of foreground and background is given in (257).

(257) Tense and aspect in ADV and WARN

		Tense		Phasal		Perfectivity			Inherent			
		FUT	NEUT	INCH	ITER	PFTV	CONT	HAB	STA	ACT	ACC	ACH
FG	ADV	1	2	0	0	3	0	0	1	2	0	0
	WARN	0	10	0	1	8	2	0	2	6	1	1
BG	ADV	8	37	2	1	40	1	3	16	14	1	4
	WARN	13	133	0	3	114	2	14	35	36	20	27
	Total	22	182	2	5	165	5	17	54	58	22	32

Apart from the chart in (257) showing that one exhortation, a foreground element, is in the future tense, note also that the phasal aspects do not play a crucial role in hortatory discourse. Sequentiality is expressed by aspectual combinations that do not include imperfectives and statives. Since (257) does not show how perfectivity and inherent aspects combine to indicate sequentiality, this is given in (258). In this table the two texts are combined and the term sequential refers to combinations like perfective activity, perfective accomplishment, and perfective achievement, while the term nonsequential refers to perfective stative, and combinations of the continuous/habitual with activity, accomplishment, and achievement. The numbers indicate number of clauses. This table shows that the foreground of hortatory discourse, as well as the background, contains both sequential and nonsequential aspectual combinations. Therefore, sequentiality is not crucial in this genre. The single occurrence of the future exhortation is significant, however, in that it shows that exhortations are not only tense-neutral. Rather, whenever exhortations are not tense-neutral, they are given in the future tense instead of the nonfuture.

(258) Sequentiality in foreground and background

	Foreground		Background	
Sequential	8	62%	83	55%
Nonsequential	5	38%	67	45%
Total	13	100%	150	100%

The ADV and WARN texts exhibit the concept of graded salience for both foreground and background. The coming together of mood, tense, and aspect to define the foreground of these texts shows that the hortatory discourse affirms the cluster concept of the foreground. These different properties are arranged on a continuum from most foregrounded to most backgrounded as shown in (259).

(259) Properties of foreground and background in ADV and WARN text

	Tense	Key aspect	Other properties
FG	tense-neutral	perfective/imperfective nonstates/states	sequential/nonsequential, imperative mood
		perfective/imperfective nonstates/states	sequential/nonsequential, hortative mood
	future	perfective/imperfective nonstates/states	sequential/nonsequential, indicative mood[50]
	nonfuture	perfective/imperfective nonstates/states	sequential/nonsequential, indicative mood[51]
BG	future/nonfuture/ tense-neutral	perfective/imperfective nonstates/states	sequential/nonsequential, indicative mood[52]

---

[50]The future sequential/nonsequential, indicative clauses are suggestions and indirect exhortations.

[51]The nonfuture sequential/nonsequential, indicative clauses are evaluations and comparisons given by the speaker to persuade the hearers.

[52]The future/nonfuture/tense-neutral sequential/nonsequential, indicative clauses are illustrations or motivations. These are the most backgrounded material, while the tense-neutral sequential/nonsequential imperative clauses are the most foregrounded material.

12
Summary and Conclusions

In this study, I have analyzed the temporal categories of tense, the perfect, and aspect in Obolo, in grammar and in the structure of discourse. In discourse structure, I have concentrated on the function of tense and aspect in grounding. The database upon which the study was based consists of four oral and six written monologue texts, representing the four main genres: narrative, procedural, expository, and hortatory.

12.1 Tense and aspect in grammar

12.1.1 Tense in grammar

Tense is here defined as locating the time of occurrence of a situation (E) sequentially relative to speech time (S), and, optionally, to one or more reference times (R^n). By relating the time of occurrence of a situation to a reference time (S or R), tense is deictic. This is expressed schematically in (260).

(260) Tense = E relative S (relative R^n).

Obolo is found to have a binary tense system with a future/nonfuture split. The future is the marked member of the system, while the nonfuture is unmarked. The language expresses the future in more than one way. There is a simple affirmative future, which is marked by the portmanteau morpheme *mV-* with a falling tone, and a simple negative future which is also marked by the falling tone prefix *kpV-*. Apart from these, there are also some modally modified futures which convey the speaker's perception of the future event. These include the definite future and the immediate future. The definite future, marked by the falling tone prefix *bV-*, conveys the speaker's assurance that the future event in question is definitely going to happen. The immediate future is marked by the prefix *mVni-*, a combination of the simple affirmative future morpheme *mV-* and the inchoative morpheme *ní-*. It conveys the speaker's belief that the event in question is about to happen.

However, *bV-* and *mVni-* do not always mark the definite and immediate future, respectively. The morpheme *bV-*, which probably grammaticized from the verb *bé-* 'say', is also used to mark intention, one of the meanings on its grammaticization path. The hybrid morpheme *mVni-* assumes its future plus inchoative meaning when it is used in conjunction with the adverb *săbùm* 'before'.

The nonfuture time has no morphological marking. The past is distinguished from the present, when necessary, by means of temporal adverbials. When a situation is perceived as generic, without any tense constraints, it is marked by the polysemous morpheme *rà*. If the situation is expressed by means of a clause chain, the prefix *rà* occurs on the first verb while other verbs carry the unneutralized subject prefixes.

12.1.2 Aspect in grammar

Aspect is defined here as expressing different ways of viewing the internal temporal constituency of a situation. Since aspect does not relate one situation to another, it is nondeictic.

Three aspectual distinctions were found in Obolo: perfectivity, inherent, and phasal aspects. The classification of aspect into three types is based on their domain of operation and their simultaneous occurrence on a single verb. While perfectivity operates at the grammatical level, both inherent and phasal aspects operate at the lexical level. While inherent aspect has to do with the inherent temporal constituency of the whole event, including phases, phasal aspects denote subsequences in the phasic structure of the event. While both perfectivity and phasal aspects are overtly marked, morphologically or periphrastically, the inherent aspect does not have any marking. Its components are distinguished on the basis of the three semantic properties: dynamicity, durativity, and telicity.

Perfectivity aspect comprises two components, perfective and imperfective. Of the three views of perfectivity in the literature, namely the temporal view, boundedness view, and totality view, the totality view accounts best for the properties of the perfective in the language. In this view, the perfective views the situation as a whole from the outside, without regard to its internal temporal constituency, while the imperfective views the situation from the inside, and is crucially concerned with the internal temporal structure of the situation. In Obolo, apart from the perfective/imperfective split, the imperfective is also split into habitual/nonhabitual. Further, the nonhabitual is split into progressive and continuous. While the perfective is unmarked, the imperfective is generally marked by the prefix *ki* on the verb. In the habitual/nonhabitual split, the habitual carries only the general imperfective marker *kí.* The continuous is optionally marked by the serial verb *kpộ/kpọ́kpộ* with the general imperfective marker *ki,* while the progressive is optionally marked by the locative prefix *gwâ* or *bâ* (singular or plural) with or without the general imperfective morpheme *ki.*

Inherent aspect consists of five components: states, activities, semelfactives, accomplishments, and achievements. States are nondynamic, inherently durative, and atelic. The only difference between activities and semelfactives is that while activities are durative, semelfactives are punctual. Otherwise, they are both dynamic and atelic. Both accomplishments and achievements are dynamic and telic. But while accomplishments are durative, achievements are punctual.

Phasal aspects, which are variously referred to as Aktionsarten (Binnick 1991) and procedurals (Forsyth 1970) in the literature, represent the classification of (or expressions for) phases of situations and subsituations (or subevents). Six types of phasal aspect are identified in the language. These include the inceptive and completive, which focus on the initial and final endpoints; the iterative and durative, which focus on the structure of the middle section of the situation; and immediative and inchoative which focus on the boundary between two situations. While the terms inceptive, completive, iterative, and durative are self-explanatory, the use of the terms immediative and inchoative require some explanations. While immediative indicates that there is no pause or temporal gap between the two situations, the inchoative indicates that there has been a change in the state of affairs, i.e., that the situation in question was not there before.

The inceptives and completives are marked periphrastically by means of the serial verbs *bénè* 'begin' and *sáñà* 'finish,' respectively. Other serial verbs also mark the completive (see chapter 5), but *sáñà* is the most frequent. The iteratives are expressed either morphologically by reduplicating the verb stem, or periphrastically by means of two serial verbs *kpọ́k* and *yákà* The morphological marking is no longer very productive in the language, so the periphrastic marking is rapidly taking over. The inchoative is marked morphologically by the prefix *ni,* in sequential contexts, and periphrastically by the serial verb *yákà,* in nonsequential contexts.

12.1.3 The perfect

The perfect here is treated as a separate temporal category. It is neither completely tense nor completely aspect. On the one hand, like tense, the perfect is deictic in the sense that it relates the time of occurrence of a situation (E) to a reference time (S/R) during which the state resulting from the situation is still relevant. This property of the perfect is not present in the meaning of aspect. On the other hand, unlike tense, the perfect expresses a state which results from a previous situation. This is the reason many linguists classify the perfect as aspect. But because of this compositional tense-plus-aspect meaning, the perfect is here classified separately, apart from tense and aspect.

The perfect in Obolo is marked by the polysemous morpheme rà which also marks genericness. The difference between the two is seen mostly in the clause chaining construction. In the perfect marking, all subsequent subject prefixes neutralize to the invariant í-, but in generic marking, they do not neutralize (see chapter 4). The perfect in Obolo marks the current relevance of a prior situation.

12.2 Tense and aspect in discourse

Hopper (1979) proposes a correlation between the perfective aspect and the narrative foreground. Also Dry (1983) proposes that it is not just perfectivity, but change-of-state (or nonstativity) that correlates with the narrative foreground. This study extends these correlations even farther. (1) The study establishes the fact that it is neither perfectivity by itself, nor change-of-state by itself, but rather a combination of sequential components from all three types of aspect, (i.e., those components which express sequentiality) that correlates with the narrative foreground. These components include the perfective from perfectivity, nonstatives from inherent aspect, and, the inchoative from phasal aspect. (2) It also establishes the fact that, as with narrative, all three aspectual distinctions contribute to the foreground of the other three major discourse genres—procedural, expository, and hortatory. (3) The study also establishes a correlation between tense and the foreground of all four discourse types.

Sequentiality, as expressed by aspect, is a crucial parameter in distinguishing between discourse types. Together with tense, it forms a useful temporal parameter by which the foreground of the four different genres may be distinguished, one from the other. Nonsequentiality is expressed by a combination of the imperfective and nonstates, and of perfective and states. Phasal aspects are not crucial in the expression of nonsequentiality.

Summary and Conclusions

In terms of these temporal structures, the foreground properties of narrative discourse tend to include nonfuture (past) time, and sequentiality, which is expressed by perfective, nonstative, and *ni* inchoative aspects. The background properties tend to include other tenses, such as future, distant past (usually indexed formulaically at the beginning of the story); and nonsequential perfective states and imperfective nonstates. But it may also include sequential aspectual components, such as the immediative, a phasal aspect component, as well as other backgrounded perfective nonstative combinations. The foreground of the procedural discourse tends to include the future tense (for procedural with projection) or nonfuture (for projectionless procedurals) and sequential perfective nonstates with *ni* inchoative. Background properties include nonfuture time and both sequential and nonsequential aspectual combinations. In the expository discourse, the foreground is tense-neutral and nonsequential, while the background tends to be tense-neutral (generic) or even future (irrealis) and both sequential and nonsequential. In the hortatory discourse the foreground consists of both future tense and tense-neutral properties, and also both sequential and nonsequential aspectual combinations. A time-based (past/present) expository compare-and-contrast text was also studied. It was found to differ from the more prototypical expository discourse by having overt marking of past and present time references, and the non sequential *yákà* inchoative in its foreground. Its background consists also of past/present time, and is both sequential and nonsequential. These properties are given in (261) and (262) for the foreground and background, respectively.

As (262) shows, sequentiality, expressed by aspects, is not a diagnostic feature in the background. The reason is that the background may contain, (1) embedded material, e.g., embedded speech in an action narrative, and embedded narratives in expository discourse; (2) repetitions, e.g., immediative in narratives and conditional clauses in procedurals; and (3) illustrative material, e.g., motivations in hortatory discourse. All of these backgrounded materials may be aspectually sequential and/or nonsequential.

One thing that (262) does not show is how tense and the different types of aspect combine, especially in the background of the narrative and procedural discourse, both of which demand high sequentiality. Neither future perfective, perfective states, nor imperfective nonstates encode sequentiality. A summary of the tense and aspect markers is given in (263).

(261) Temporal properties of the foreground

Property	Narrative	Procedural	Expository	Compare/Contrast	Hortatory
Tense	Nonfuture (past)	Alpha future: Future (+projection) Nonfuture (-projection)	Tense-neutral (generic)	Past/Present (for time-based contrast)	Tense-neutral or Future
Sequentiality (expressed by aspects)	Sequential	Sequential	Nonsequential	Nonsequential	Both sequential and nonsequential
Aspect Perfectivity	Perfective	Perfective	Imperfective (HAB)	Imperfective	Perfective, Imperfective
Inherent	Nonstative	Nonstative	Stative	Stative	Stative, Nonstative
Phasal	Inchoative (-ni-)	Inchoative (-ni-)	(Not diagnostic)	Inchoative (-yákà)	(Not diagnostic)

Summary and Conclusions

(262) Temporal properties of the background

Property	Narrative	Procedural	Expository	Compare/Contrast	Hortatory
Tense	Future Distant past (by formulaic expression) Tense-neutral	Nonfuture: (both +projection and -projection)	Tense-neutral (generic) and/or Future (irrealis)	Past/Present (for time-based contrast)	Both Nonfuture and Future
Sequentiality (expressed by aspects)	Both sequential and nonsequential (Not diagnostic)	Both sequential and nonsequential (Not diagnostic)	Both sequential and nonsequential (Not diagnostic)	Both sequential and nonsequential (Not diagnostic)	Both sequential and nonsequential (Not diagnostic)
Aspect: Perfectivity	Perfective, Imperfective	Perfective, Imperfective	Perfective, Imperfective	Perfective, Imperfective	Perfective, Imperfective
Inherent	Stative, Nonstative	Stative, Nonstative	Stative, Nonstative	Stative, Nonstative	Stative, Nonstative
Phasal	Immediacy	(Not diagnostic)	(Not diagnostic)	(Not diagnostic)	(Not diagnostic)

(263) Summary of tense and aspect markers

Category			Marker Affirmative	Negative
Tense				
Future:				
Simple	1sg		mâ-	kpâ-
	2/3sg		mô-	kpô-
	cpl		mê-	kpê-
Definite	1sg		bâ-	kpá-bâ-
	2/3sg		bô-	kpó-bô-
	cpl		bê-	kpè-bê-
Immediate	1sg		mâ-nĭ-	∅
	2/3sg		mô-nĭ-	∅
	cpl		mê-nĭ-	∅
Nonfuture			∅	kâ- (sg)
				kpĕ- (pl)
Perfect:			rà-/ràbí-	kâ/kpĕ + rà/ràbí
Aspect				
Perfectivity				
Perfective			∅	kâ/kpĕ + ∅
Imperfective				
Habitual			-kí-	ká + kì-
				kpè + kí-
Progressive	sg		(gwâ) + -kí-	∅
	pl		(bâ) + -kí-	∅
Continuous			kpó/kpókpộ (+ kí-)	kâ/kpĕ + kpó/kpókpộ + kí-
Inherent			∅	kâ/kpĕ
Phasal				
Inceptive			-bénè	kâ/kpĕ + béné
Completive			-sáñà/ràká/kèm	kâ/kpĕ + sáñá/ràká/kèm
Durative			repetition	kâ/kpĕ +repetition
			mégê/àbáyàgê	kâ/kpĕ + mégê/àbáyàgê
Iterative			stem redup.	kâ/kpĕ + stem redup.
			yáká/kpók	kâ/kpĕ + yáká/kpók
Immediative			redup	∅
Inchoative			-ní-/nèní-	kâ/kpĕ +yáká

12.3 Conclusions

The choice of tense and aspect is discourse motivated, but with the consideration of the sentential semantic meaning of the specific tense or aspect.

All monologue discourse has some sort of relational structure in which some portions are highlighted or foregrounded, while others (background) perform corroborative functions. The properties of the foreground are different depending on the type of discourse. In Obolo, each of the three types of aspect contributes to the properties of the foreground and background. For instance, in terms of aspect, the foreground of the narrative WB text consists mainly of perfective, (inchoative), nonstative events, while the foreground of the nonnarrative PROGS text consists mainly of imperfective, stative situations. These properties are exact opposites of each other.

The foreground is a cluster concept, comprising multiple properties all of which need not be present for the definition of the foreground. The foreground/background distinction is seen to be a scalar continuum rather than a binary opposition. The continuum consists of typical foreground properties at one end, typical background properties at the other end, and a mixture of properties in the middle.

The function of these grammatical categories of tense and aspect in diagnostically shaping the structure of the different discourse genres is clear evidence that discourse motivates grammar.

Appendix

Affirmative verb patterns

This table shows how aspect, perfect, and tense interact with mood and focus to give the different affirmative verb patterns in the language. V = Verb Focus, AP = Auxiliary Focus (Imperfective), AC = Auxiliary Focus (Inchoative), AS = Auxiliary Focus (Subjunctive), PrF = Prefocus, PsF = Postfocus, INF = Infinitive, HTV = High Tone Verb, LTV = Low Tone Verb, FU = Future, IFU = Immediate Future, PDFU = Definite Future in the Past, NF = Nonfuture, SJREL = Subject Relativized Relative Clause, GEN = Generic. Under Stem Tone column, 1 = CV verb syllable pattern, 2 = CVC, 3 = CVCV. All other abbreviations are as given in the abbreviations section in the work. When not spelled out, the 1st and 2nd subject prefixes are n- and o-, respectively, only tone changes are indicated in such instances.

Pattern No.	Aspect/Mood	Tense Focus	AuxPref	1 & 2 sg SP Tone	Subject Prefix 3s	Subject Prefix cpl	Prefix Marker	REDUP SYL. Tone HTV	REDUP SYL. Tone LTV	Stem Tone HTV 1	Stem Tone HTV 2	Stem Tone HTV 3	Stem Tone LTV 1	Stem Tone LTV 2	Stem Tone LTV 3	Suff
1	PFTV INF	v						HL	HL	L	L	LL	L	L	LL	
2	IMPF INF	AP	í							H	L	HL	H	L	LH	
3	IMPF INF	AP/v	í					H	L	HL	HL	HL	HL	HL	HL	
4	PFTV IMP	✓	í							HL	HL	HL	LHL	HL	HL	
5	PFTV IMP	v	í							HL	HL	HL	HL	HL	HL	
6	IMPF IMP	✓			í		kí/kí (s/p)			HL	HL	HL	LHL	HL	HL	
7	IMPF IMP	v			í		kí/kí (s/p)			HL	HL	HL	HL	HL	HL	
8	PFTV HORT	✓		L	í	è	kí/kí			HL	HL	HL	HL	HL	HL	
9	PFTV HORT	v		L	í	è	kí/kí			HL	HL	HL	HL	HL	HL	
10	IMPF HORT	✓		L	í	è	kò/kí			HL	HL	HL	HL	HL	HL	
11	IMPF HORT	v		L	í	è	kò/kí	H		HL	HL	HL	HL	HL	HL	
12	PFTV SBJ	✓	kè	L/H(HTV/LTV)	ò/ó	è/é		H	L	HL	HL	LL	L	L	LL	
13	PFTV SBJ	v	kè	L/H(HTV/LTV)	ò/ó	è/é		H	L	HL	HL	HL	HL	HL	HL	
14	IMPF SBJ	✓	kè	L	ò/ó	è/é	kò/kó (HTV/LTV)	H	L	HL	HL	HL	L	L	LL	
15	IMPF SBJ	v	kè	L	ò/ó	è/é	kò/kó (HTV/LTV)	H	L	HL	HL	HL	HL	HL	HL	
16	PFTV SBJ	AS	kèkè	L	ò/ó	è/é		H		HL	HL	HL	HL	HL	HL	
17	PFTV SBJ	AS/v	kèkè	L	ò	è		H	L	HL	HL	HL	L	L	LL	
18	IMPF SBJ	AS	kèkè	L	ò	è	kò/kó(HTV/LTV)	H		HL	HL	HL	HL	HL	HL	
19	IMPF SBJ	AS/v	kèkè	L	ò	è	kè/kò/kóké	H	H	HL	HL	HL	HL	HL	HL	
20	PFTV SBJ COND	✓	kè	H (má/mó)	mó	mé		H		H	H	HH	H	H	LH	
21	PFTV SBJ COND	v	kè	H (má/mó)	mó	mé		H	L	HL	HL	HL	HL	HL	HL	
22	IMPF SBJ COND	✓	kè	H (má/mó)	mó	mé	kí	H		H	H	HH	H	H	LH	
23	IMPF SBJ COND	v	kè	H (má/mó)	mó	mé	kí	H	L	HL	HL	HL	HL	HL	HL	
24	PFTV PERF SBJ	✓	kè -rà	H	ó	mí		H		H	H	HH	H	H	LH	

Appendix

Pattern No.	Aspect/Mood	Tense	Focus	AuxPref	1 & 2 sg sp Tone	Subject Prefix 3s	Subject Prefix cpl	Prefix Marker	REDUP syl. Tone HTV	REDUP syl. Tone LTV	Stem Tone HTV 1	Stem Tone HTV 2	Stem Tone HTV 3	Stem Tone LTV 1	Stem Tone LTV 2	Stem Tone LTV 3	Suff
25	PFTV PERF SBJ		v	kè -rà	H	ì	mî		H		HL	H	HL	HL	HL	HL	HL
26	IMPF PERF SBJ		/	kè -rà	H	ì	mî					H	H	HL	H	L	LH
27	IMPF PERF SBJ		v	kè -rà	H	ì	mî					H	HL	HL	HL	HL	HL
28	PFTV COND	NF	/		H (má/mó)	mó	mê	kî	H		HL	HL	HH	HL	HL	HL	HL
29	PFTV COND	NF	v		H (má/mó)	mó	mê	kî				H	HH	HL	H	L	LH
30	IMPF COND	NF	/		H (má/mó)	mó	mê					HL	HH	HL	HL	HL	HL
31	IMPF COND	NF	v		H (má/mó)	mó	mê	kî	H		HL	HL	HH	HL	HL	HL	HL
32	PFTV IND	FU	/		HL (má/mó)	mó	mê	kî		L	L	L	LL	HL	L	L	LL
33	PFTV IND	FU	v		HL (má/mó)	mó	mê	kî			HL	HL	HL	HL	HL	HL	HL
34	IMPF IND	FU	/		HL (má/mó)	mó	mê	kî				H	HH	HL	H	L	LH
35	IMPF IND	FU	v		HL (má/mó)	mó	mê	kî	H		HL	HL	HL	HL	HL	HL	HL
36	PFTV IND	DFU	/		L	ì	è	bV		L	L	L	LL	L	L	L	LL
37	PFTV IND	DFU	v		L (má/mó)	ì	è	bV	L		HL	HL	HH	HL	HL	HL	HL
38	IMPF IND	DFU	/		L (má/mó)	ì	è	bV+kî				H	HH	HL	H	L	LH
39	IMPF IND	DFU	v		L (má/mó)	ì	è	bV+kî	H		HL	HL	HL	HL	HL	HL	HL
40	PFTV IND	IFU	/		HL (má/mó)	mó	mê	mV+nî				H	HH	HL	H	H	HL
41	PFTV IND	IFU	v		HL (má/mó)	mó	mê	mV+nî	H		HL	HL	HL	HL	HL	HL	HL
42	IMPF IND	IFU	/		HL (má/mó)	mó	mê	mV+nî+kî				H	HH	HL	H	L	LH
43	IMPF IND	IFU	v		HL (má/mó)	mó	mê	mV+nî+kî	H		HL	HL	HL	HL	HL	HL	HL
44	PFTV COND	DFU	/		H (má/mó)	mó	mê	mV+bV		L	L	L	LL	L	L	L	LL
45	PFTV COND	DFU	v		H (má/mó)	mó	mê	mV+bV	L		HL	HL	HL	HL	HL	HL	HL
46	IMPF COND	DFU	/		H (má/mó)	mó	mê	mV+bV+kî				H	HH	HL	H	L	LH
47	IMPF COND	DFU	v		H (má/mó)	mó	mê	mV+bV+kî	H		HL	HL	HL	HL	HL	HL	HL

Pattern No.	Aspect/Mood	Tense	Focus	Aux Pref	1 & 2 sg SP Tone	Subject Prefix 3s	cpl	Prefix Marker	REDUP SYL. Tone HTV / LTV	Stem Tone HTV 1 2 3	LTV 1 2 3	L T V 1 2 3	Suff
48	PFTV COND INCH	DFU	/		H (má/mó)	mó	mé	mV+bV+nĭ		H H HH	H H HH	H L HL	HL
49	PFTV COND INCH	DFU	v		H (má/mó)	mó	mé	mV+bV+nĭ	H	HL HL HL	HL HL HL	HL L HL	LH
50	IMPF COND INCH	DFU	/		H (má/mó)	mó	mé	mV+bV+nĭ+kí		H H HH	H H HH	H L HL	HL
51	IMPF COND INCH	DFU	v		H (má/mó)	mó	mé	mV+bV+nĭ+kí	H	HL HL HL	HL HL HL	HL L HL	LH
52	PFTV IND INCH	DFU	/		L	ĭ	é	bV + nĭ		H H HH	H H HH	H L HL	HL
53	PFTV IND INCH	DFU	v		L	ĭ	é	bV + nĭ	H	HL HL HL	HL HL HL	HL L HL	LH
54	IMPF IND INCH	DFU	/		L	ĭ	é	bV+nĭ+kí		H H HH	H H HH	H L HL	LL
55	IMPF IND INCH	DFU	v		L	ĭ	é	bV+nĭ+kí	H	HL HL HL	HL HL HL	HL L HL	LH bé
56	PFTV IND REL	FU	/		HL (má/mó)	mó	mé	mV-		HL HL HL	HL HL HL	HL L HL	LL bé
57	PFTV IND REL	NF	v		H	ĭ	é			L L LL	L L LL	L L L	LH
58	PFTV IND	NF	/		H	ĭ	mí		L	L L LL	L L LL	L LH LH	HL
59	PFTV IND	NF	v		H	ĭ	mí			HL HL HL	HL HL HL	HL LH HL	HL
60	PFTV IND	NF	PSF		L	ĭ	é		L	HL HL HH	HL HL HH	HL LH HL	LH
61	PFTV IND	NF	v		L	ĭ	é			HL HL HL	HL HL HL	HL H HL	HL
62	PFTV IND	NF	PSF		H	ó	é		H	H H HH	H H HH	H LH HL	LH
63	IMPF IND	NF	/		H	ĭ	é	kí/kì		L L LL	L L LL	LH H HL	HL
64	IMPF IND	NF	v		H	ĭ	é	kí/kì	L	L L LL	L L LL	LH LH HL	HL
65	IMPF IND	NF	PSV		L	ĭ	é	kí		H H HH	H H HH	H LH HL	HL
66	IMPF IND	NF	v		L	ĭ	é	kí/kí		HL HL HL	HL HL HL	HL H HL	HL
67	IMPF IND	NF	AP		L	ĭ	é	kèkí		HL HL HL	HL HL HL	HL H HL	HL
68	IMPF IND	NF	PTF		L	ó	é	kí	H	HL HL HL	HL HL HL	HL H HL	HL
69	IMPF IND	NF	PTF/V		H	ó	é	kí		HL HL HL	HL HL HL	HL H HL	HL
70	IMPF (PROG) IND	NF	/	gwâ/bâ	L	ò	mé		H	H H HH	H H HH	H L HL	LH
71	IMPF (PROG) IND	NF	/	gwâ/bâ	L/H	ò	mé		L	HL HL HL	HL HL HL	HL L HL	LL

Pattern No.	Aspect/Mood	Tense	Focus	Aux Pref rà/ràbí	1 & 2 sg sp Tone	Subject Prefix 3s	cpl	Prefix Marker	REDUP SYL Tone HTV	LTV	Stem Tone HTV 1	2	3	LTV 1	2	3	Suff
72	PFTV PERF IND	NF	/	rà/ràbí	H	í	mí				H	H	HH	H	L	HL	LH
73	PFTV PERF IND	NF	v	rà/ràbí	H	í	mí				HL	HL	HH	HL	L	HL	LH
74	PFTV PERF INCH IND	NF	/	rà/ràbí	H	í	mí	ní	H		H	H	HH	H	L	HL	LH
75	PFTV PERF INCH IND	NF	v	rà/ràbí	H	í	mí	ní	H		HL	HL	HH	HL	L	HL	LH
76	IMPF PERF IND	NF	/	rà/ràbí	H	í	mí	kí	H		H	H	HH	H	L	HL	LH
77	IMPF PERF IND	NF	v	rà/ràbí	H	í	mí	kí	H		HL	HL	HH	HL	L	HL	LH
78	IMPF PERF INCH IND	NF	/	rà/ràbí	H	í	mí	ní+kí			H	H	HH	H	L	HL	LH
79	IMPF PERF INCH IND	NF	v	rà/ràbí	H	í	mí	ní+kí			HL	HL	HH	HL	L	HL	LH
80	PFTV INCH IND	NF	/		H	ì	é	ní			H	H	HH	H	L	HL	LH
81	PFTV INCH IND	NF	PSF		L	ì	é	ní			HL	HL	HL	HL	L	HL	HL
82	PFTV INCH IND	NF	PSF		L	ì	é	ní			HL	HL	HL	HL	L	HL	HL
83	PFTV INCH IND	NF	PtF		L	ò	è	nì			HL	HL	HL	HL	L	HL	HL
84	PFTV INCH HORT	NF	AF		H	í	é	!nênI			HL	HL	HL	HL	L	HL	HL
85	PFTV INCH IND	NF	PtF/AC		H	ó	é	!nênI			HL	HL	HL	HL	L	HL	HL
86	PFTV INCH IND	NF	PtF/v		H	ó	é	!nênI			HL	HL	HL	HL	L	HL	HL
87	IMPF INCH IND	NF	/		H	í	é	ní+kí	H		HL	HL	HL	HL	L	HL	HL
88	IMPF INCH IND	NF	PSF		L	ì	é	ní+kí			HL	HL	HL	HL	L	HL	HL
89	IMPF INCH IND	NF	PtF		H	ó	é	ní+kí			HL	HL	HL	HL	L	HL	HL
90	IMPF INCH HORT	NF	PtF		L	ò	é	nù/ní+kà/kí			HL	HL	HL	HL	L	HL	HL
91	IMPF INCH IND	NF	AC		H	í	é	!nênI+kí			HL	HL	HL	HL	L	HL	HL
92	IMPF INCH IND	NF	PtF/AC		H	ó	é	!nênI+kí			HL	HL	HL	HL	L	HL	HL
93	IMPF INCH IND	NF	PtF/AC/v		H	ó	é	!nênI+kí	H	L	HL	HL	HL	HL	L	HL	HL
94	PFTV INCH IND	NF	v		H	í	é	ní	H	L	HL	HL	HL	HL	L	HL	HL

170   Tense and Aspect in Obolo Grammar and Discourse

Pattern No.	Aspect/Mood	Tense	Focus	Aux Pref 1 & 2 sg SP Tone	Subject Prefix 3s	Subject Prefix cpl	Prefix Marker	REDUP syl. Tone HTV	REDUP syl. Tone LTV	Stem Tone HTV 1	HTV 2	HTV 3	Stem Tone LTV 1	LTV 2	LTV 3	Suff 3
95	PFTV INCH IND	NF	PSF/V	L	ɔ̀	e	nɪ́	H	L	HL	HL	HL	HL	HL	HL	HL
96	PFTV INCH IND	NF	PTF/V	H	ó	e	ɪ́nɪ́	H	L	HL	HL	HL	HL	HL	HL	HL
97	PFTV INCH HORT		V	L	ɔ̀	ə	nɪ̀	H	L	HL	HL	HL	HL	HL	HL	HL
98	IMPF INCH HORT		V	L	ɔ̀	ə	nɪ̀+kɪ́	H	L	HL	HL	HL	HL	HL	HL	HL
99	IMPF INCH IND	NF	V	H	í	e	nɪ́+kɪ́	H	L	HL	HL	HL	HL	HL	HL	HL
100	IMPF INCH IND	NF	PSF/V	L	ɔ̀	e	nɪ́+kɪ́	H	L	HL	HL	HL	HL	HL	HL	HL
101	IMPF INCH IND	NF	PTF/V	H	ó	e	nɪ́+kɪ́	H	L	HL	HL	HL	HL	HL	HL	LH
102	PFTV INCH IND	NF	PTF	H	ó	e	ɪ́nɪ́		L	H	H	H	HL	L	L	LH
103	PFTV INCH IND	NF	PTF/V	H	ó	e	ɪ́nɪ́		L	HL	HL	HH	HL	HL	HL	LH
104	IMPF INCH IND	NF	PTF	H	ó	e	ɪ́nɪ́+kɪ́	H	L	H	H	HH	HL	HL	HL	HL
105	IMPF INCH IND	NF	PTF/V	H	ó	e	ɪ́nɪ́+kɪ́		L	HL	HL	HL	HL	HL	HL	L
106	IMPF IND	NF	AP	H	í	e	!kéki	H	L	H	H	HH	HL	HL	HL	HL
107	IMPF IND	NF	AP/V	H	í	e	!kéki	L	L	L	L	LL	HL	L	L	LL
108	IMPF IND	PDFU	AP	H	í	e	!kéki+bó	L	L	HL	HL	HL	HL	HL	HL	HL
109	IMPF IND	PDFU	AP/V	H	í	e	!kéki+bó		L	H	H	HH	HL	HL	HL	LH
110	IMPF INCH IND	PDFU	AP	H	í	e	!kéki+bó+nɪ́	H	L	L	L	LL	L	L	L	L
111	IMPF INCH IND	PDFU	AP	H	í	e	!kéki+bó+ɪ́		ꜛHL	HL	HL	HL	HL	HL	HL	HL
112	PFTV IND	NF	V	L	ɔ̀				ꜛHL	L	L	L	HL	HL	HL	L
113	PFTV IND SJ REL	NF	/	L	ɔ̀		kɪ́	HL	HL	L	L	LL	HL	L	L	LL
114	PFTV IND SJ REL	NF	V	L	ɔ̀		kɪ́		L	L	L	LL	HL	L	L	LH
115	IMPF IND SJ REL	NF	/	H	í		sɪ́		L	H	H	HH	H	H	H	HL
116	IMPF IND SJ REL	NF	V	H	í		sɪ́		L	H	H	HH	HL	HL	HL	LH
117	PFTV CNS	GEN	/													
118	PFTV CNS	GEN	V					H	L	HL	HL	HL	HL	HL	HL	HL

Appendix

Pattern No.	Aspect/Mood	Tense	Focus	Aux Pref	1 & 2 sg SP Tone	Subject Prefix 3s	Subject Prefix cpl	Prefix Marker	REDUP SYL. Tone HTV	REDUP SYL. Tone LTV	Stem Tone HTV 1	Stem Tone HTV 2	Stem Tone HTV 3	Stem Tone LTV 1	Stem Tone LTV 2	Stem Tone LTV 3	Suff
119	IMPF CNS	GEN	/			í											
120	IMPF CNS	GEN	V		H	í		sĭ+kí			H	H	HH	HL	H	L	LH
121	PFTV CNS INCH	GEN	/		H	í		sĭ+kí			HL	HL	HL	HL	HL	HL	HL
122	PFTV CNS INCH	GEN	V		H	í		sĭ+ní			H	H	HH	HL	H	L	LH
123	IMPF CNS INCH	GEN	/		H	í		sĭ+ní			HL	HL	HL·	HL	HL	HL	HL
124	IMPF CNS INCH	GEN	V		H	í		sĭ+ní+kí			H	H	HH	HL	H	L	LH
125	IMPF (PROG) IND	NF	V	gwá/bá	L	ò		sĭ+ní+kí	H	L	HL	HL	HL	HL	HL	HL	HL
126	IMPF (PROG) IND	NF	V	gwá/bá	L	ò		kí	H	L	HL	HL	HL	HL	HL	HL	HL
127	PFTV IND	FU	V		HL	mô	mê	/	!HL	!HL	L	L	LL	L	L	L	LL
128	PFTV INCH IND	FU	AC		HL	mô	mê	nênĭ	H	L	H	H	HH	HL	H	L	LH
129	PFTV INCH IND	FU	AC/V		HL	mô	mê	nênĭ			HL	HL	HL	HL	HL	HL	HL
130	IMPF INCH IND	FU	AC		HL	mô	mê	nênĭ+kí			H	H	HH	HL	H	L	LH
131	IMPF INCH IND	FU	AC/V		HL	mô	mê	nênĭ+kí			HL	HL	HL	HL	HL	HL	HL
132	IMPF IND	FU	AP		HL	mô	mê	!kêkĭ	H	L	H	H	HH	HL	H	L	LH
133	IMPF IND	FU	AP/V		HL	mô	mê	!kêkĭ			HL	HL	HL	HL	HL	HL	HL

HTV examples of the verb patterns

The numbers correspond to the pattern numbers in the chart. All examples are of the high tone verb *sí* 'go'.[53]

1.	ísîsí	to go
2.	íkêkǐsí	to be going
3.	íkêkǐsísî	to be GOING
4.	sî	go
5.	sísî	GO
6.	kísî	be going
7.	kísísî	be GOING
8.	ísî	let him/her go
9.	ísísî	let him/her GO
10.	íkísî	let him/her be going
11.	íkísísî	let him/her be GOING
12.	kè òsî	s/he should go
13.	kè òsísî	s/he should GO
14.	kè òkòsî	s/he should be going
15.	kè òkòsísî	s/he should be GOING
16.	kékè òsî	s/he SHOULD go
17.	kékè òsísî	s/he SHOULD GO
18.	kékè òkòsî	s/he SHOULD be going
19.	kékè òkòsísî	s/he SHOULD be GOING
20.	kè mósí	s/he would go
21.	kè mósísî	s/he would GO
22.	kè mókísí	s/he would be going
23.	kè mókísísî	s/he would be GOING
24.	kè îrà ísí	s/he would have gone
25.	kè îrà ísísî	s/he would have GONE
26.	kè îrà íkísí	s/he would have been going
27.	kè îrà íkísísî	s/he would have been GOING
28.	mósí	if s/he went
29.	mósísî	if s/he WENT
30.	mókísí	if s/he were going
31.	mókísísî	if s/he were GOING
32.	môsì	s/he will go
33.	môsìsî	s/he will GO
34.	môkǐsí	s/he will be going

---

[53] The reader is advised to refer to the chart as he reads the examples. There is no space here to label the examples for aspect, perfect, tense, mood, and focus; these are already done in the chart. Low tone verb examples are not given, eg., the verb *tàp* 'put'. Their tone patterns are given in the chart for a guide.

Appendix

35.	môkǐsísî	s/he will be GOING
36.	ìbôsì	s/he is going to go
37.	ìbôsìsî	s/he is going to GO
38.	ìbôkǐsì	s/he is going to be going
39.	ìbôkǐsìsî	s/he is going to be GOING
40.	mônǔsí	s/he is about to go
41.	mônǔsísî	s/he is about to GO
42.	mônǐkísí	s/he is about to be going
43.	mônǐkísísî	s/he is about to be GOING
44.	móbôsì	when s/he will intend to go
45.	móbôsìsî	when s/he will intend to GO
46.	móbôkǐsí	when s/he will intend to be going
47.	móbôkǐsísî	when s/he will intend to be GOING
48.	móbônǔsí	now/then when s/he will intend to go
49.	móbônǔsísî	now/then when s/he will intend to GO
50.	móbônǐkísí	now/then when s/he will intend to be going
51.	móbônǐkísísî	now/then when s/he will intend to be GOING
52.	ìbônǔsí	s/he intends to go...
53.	ìbônǔsísî	s/he intends to GO...
54.	ìbônǐkísí	s/he intends to be going...
55.	ìbônǐkísísî	s/he intends to be GOING...
56.	môsǐbé	the place(or time) s/he would go (one who would go)
57.	îsìbé	place/when s/he went
58.	îsì	s/he went
59.	îsìsî	s/he WENT and...
60.	ìsí	s/he went to...
61.	ìsísî	s/he WENT (not returned)
62.	ósí	S/HE went
63.	íkìsì	s/he habitually goes
64.	íkìsìsî	s/he habitually GOES
65.	ìkísí	s/he habitually goes to...
66.	ìkísísî	s/he habitually GOES to...
67.	ìkékísí	s/he HABITUALLY goes to...
68.	ókísí	S/HE habitually goes
69.	ókísísî	S/HE habitually GOES
70.	ògwâ òkísí	s/he is/was going
71.	ògwâ òsî	s/he is/was going
72.	îrà ísí	s/he has gone
73.	îrà ísísî	s/he has GONE
74.	îrà ínísí	s/he has now/then gone
75.	îrà ínísísî	s/he has now/then GONE

76.	ìrà íkísí	s/he has been going
77.	ìrà íkísísî	s/he has been GOING
78.	ìrà ínîkísí	s/he has now been going
79.	ìrà ínîkísísî	s/he has now been GOING
80.	ínísí	s/he then went (serial form)
81.	ìnísí	s/he now/then went to...
82.	ónísí	S/HE now/then went
83.	ònòsî	(so that) S/HE go (lit. (so that) let HIM/HER go)
84.	í!nênǐsí	THEN s/he went
85.	ó!nênǐsí	THEN S/HE went
86.	ó!nênísísî	THEN S/HE WENT
87.	ínîkísí	s/he now/then is/was going (serial form)
88.	ìnîkísí	s/he now/then is/was going to...
89.	ónîkísí	S/HE now/then is/was going
90.	ònòkòsî	(so that) S/HE be going (lit. (so that) let HIM/HER be going)
91.	í!nênǐkísí	THEN s/he was going
92.	ó!nênǐkísí	THEN S/HE was going
93.	ó!nênǐkísísî	THEN S/HE was GOING
94.	ínísísî	s/he then WENT (serial form)
95.	ìnísísî	s/he now/then WENT...
96.	ó!nísísî	then S/HE WENT
97.	ònòsísî	(so that) S/HE GOES (lit. (so that) let HIM/HER GO)
98.	ònòkòsísî	(so that) S/HE be GOING (lit. (...) let HIM/HER be GOING)
99.	ínîkísísî	s/he then was going (serial form)
100.	ìnîkísísî	s/he then was GOING (serial form)
101.	ónîkísísî	S/HE then was going
102.	ó!nísí	S/HE then went
103.	ó!nísísî	S/HE then WENT
104.	ó!nîkísí	S/HE then was going
105.	ó!nîkísísî	S/HE then was GOING
106.	í!kêkìsí	then s/he WAS going
107.	í!kêkìsísî	then s/he WAS GOING
108.	í!kêkìbôsì	then s/he WAS going to go
109.	í!kêkìbôsìsî	then s/he WAS going to be GOING
110.	í!kêkìbônǐsí	then s/he WAS intending to be going
111.	í!kêkìbônǐsísî	then s/he WAS intending to be GOING
112.	í!sêsì	then s/he went
113.	òsî	ONE who went
114.	òsîsì	ONE who WENT

115.	òkísì	ONE who goes
116.	òkísìsî	ONE who GOES
117.	ísísí	whenever s/he goes
118.	ísísísî	whenever s/he GOES
119.	ísíkísí	whenever s/he is going
120.	ísíkísísî	whenever s/he is GOING
121.	ísínísí	then whenever s/he goes
122.	ísínísísî	then whenever s/he GOES
123.	ísíníkísí	then whenever s/he is going
124.	ísíníkísísî	then whenever s/he is GOING
125.	ògwâ òkísísî	s/he is GOING
126.	ògwâ òsísî	s/he is GOING
127.	mô!sísì	then s/he will GO
128.	mô!nênìsí	THEN s/he will go
129.	mô!nênìsísî	THEN s/he will GO
130.	mô!nênìkísí	THEN s/he will be going
131.	mô!nênìkísísî	THEN s/he will be GOING
132.	mô!kêkìsí	then s/he WILL BE going
133.	mô!kêkìsísî	then s/he WILL BE GOING

Negative verb patterns

The NEG markers are *kà-* (with NF/IFU sg), *kà-* + *-bé/gè* (for sg/pl rel. verbs), and *kpV-* everywhere else. Morphological marking of negation on the verb has some restrictions. It does not occur with the following categories: subjunctive *kè/kéké*, conditional DFU, *ní-* INCH constructions (see section 6.3.6), progressive verbs, *!kêkí* and Dstem narrative verb forms, all AUX, focus forms, all pre/post focus forms, as well as all consequential verb forms. Negative infinitive is the same form as that used for relativized post-verbal form. The iterative marker *yaka* is reduced to just *y* in fast speech resulting in novel verb forms like *ìkáyìkìsí* (s/he does not go anymore) instead of *ìkàyáká ìkìsí*, and *ìkpôyítàp* (s/he will not put anymore) instead of *ìkpôyáká ítàp*. This defective negative form is not included in the chart. DEL-NEG = delayed negative (i.e., not yet).

Pattern No.	Aspect/Mood	Tense Focus	Aux Pref	1 & 2 sg SP Tone	Subject Prefix 3s	Subject Prefix cpl	Prefix Marker	REDUP SYL. Tone HTV	REDUP SYL. Tone LTV	Stem Tone HTV 1	Stem Tone HTV 2	Stem Tone HTV 3	Stem Tone LTV 1	Stem Tone LTV 2	Stem Tone LTV 3	Suff
1	PFTV INF		é				kà			HL	H	HH	HL	HL	HL	bè / gè
2	IMPF INF	∨	ɛ̀kàkīɓɛ̀/gè	L	ɲ̀	ɲ̀		H	L	H	H	HH	LH	LH	LH	
3	IMPF INF	∨	ɛ̀kàkīɓɛ̀/gè	L	ɲ̀	ɲ̀				HL	HL	HL	LH	LH	HL	
4	PFTV IMP	/				í	kà			H	H	HH	LH	LH	HL	
5	PFTV IMP	∨				í	kà	H	L	HL	HL	HL	LH	LH	HL	
6	IMPF IMP	/				ɲ̀	kà kí			H	H	HH	LH	LH	HL	
7	IMPF IMP	∨				ɲ̀	kà kí	H	L	HL	HL	HL	LH	LH	HL	
8	PFTV HORT	/		H		é	kà			H	H	HH	LH	LH	HL	
9	PFTV HORT	∨		H		é	kà	H	L	HL	HL	HL	LH	LH	HL	
10	IMPF HORT	/		H		é	kà/kí			H	H	HH	H	L	LH	
11	IMPF HORT	∨		H		é	kà/kí	H	L	HL	HL	HL	H	L	HL	
12	PFTV COND	/	kpà/kpò/kpè	H (má/mó)	mó	mé				H	H	HH	LH	LH	HL	
13	PFTV COND	∨	kpà/kpò/kpè	H (má/mó)	mó	mé		H	L	HL	HL	HL	LH	LH	HL	
14	IMPF COND	/	kpà/kpò/kpè	H (má/mó)	mó	mé	kí			H	H	HH	H	L	LH	
15	IMPF COND	∨	kpà/kpò/kpè	H (má/mó)	mó	mé	kí	H	L	HL	HL	HL	H	L	HL	
16	PFTV IND	/		L (ḿ/ò)	ɲ̀	∅	kpâ/kpô/kpê			HL	HL	HL	HL	HL	HL	
17	PFTV IND	∨		L (ḿ/ò)	ɲ̀	∅	kpà/kpò/kpè	H	L	HL	HL	HL	HL	HL	HL	
18	IMPF IND	/		L (ḿ/ò)	ɲ̀	∅	kpà/kpò/kpê+kí			HL	H	HH	HL	HL	LH	
19	IMPF IND	∨		L (ḿ/ò)	ɲ̀	∅	kpà/kpò/kpê+kí	H	L	HL	HL	HL	H	L	HL	
20	PFTV IND	/		L (ḿ/ò)	ɲ̀	∅	kà/kpà/kpò/kpè + bV (HL)			LL	L	LL	L	L	LL	

Appendix

Pattern No.	Aspect/Mood	Tense Focus	Aux Pref	1 & 2 sg SP Tone	Subject Prefix 3s	Subject Prefix cpl	Prefix Marker	REDUP SYL Tone HTV	REDUP SYL Tone LTV	Stem Tone HTV 1	Stem Tone HTV 2	Stem Tone HTV 3	Stem Tone LTV 1	Stem Tone LTV 2	Stem Tone LTV 3	Suff
21	PFTV IND	DFU	v	L (m̀/ò)	ì	∅	ká/kpá/kpó/kpè +bV (HL)		L	HL	HL	HL	HL	HL	HL	
22	IMPF IND	DFU	/	L (m̀/ò)	ì	∅	ká/kpá/kpó/kpè +bV (HL)			H	H	HH	H	L	LH	
23	IMPF IND	DFU	v	L (m̀/ò)	ì	é	ká/kpá/kpó/kpè +bV (HL) + kí	H	L	HL	HL	HL	HL	HL	HL	
24	PFTV IND INCH	DFU	/	L	ì	∅	ká/kpá/kpó/kpè +bV (HL) + kí			H	H	HH	H	L	LH	
25	PFTV IND INCH	DFU	v	L	ì	∅	ká/kpá/kpó/kpè +bV (HL) + ní	H	L	HL	HL	HL	HL	HL	HL	
26	IMPF IND INCH	DFU	/	L	ì	∅	ká/kpá/kpó/kpè +bV (HL) + ní				H	HH		H	LL	
27	IMPF IND INCH	DFU	v	L	ì	∅	ká/kpá/kpó/kpè +bV + ní + kí	H	L	HL	HL	HL	HL	HL	HL	
28	PFTV IND REL	FU	/	L	ì	∅	kpá/kpó/kpè			HL	HL	HL	HL	HL	HL	
29	PFTV IND REL	NF	/	H	í	é	kà			HL	HL	HL	HL	HL	HL	bé
30	PFTV IND	NF	/	L	ì	∅	ká/kpé			H	H	HH	LH	LH	LH	bé
31	PFTV IND	NF	v	L	ì	∅	ká/kpé	H	L	HL	HL	HL	HL	HL	HL	
32	IMPF IND	NF	/	L	ì	∅	ká/kpè + kì/kí			HL	HL	HL	HL	HL	HL	
33	IMPF IND	NF	v	L	ì	∅	ká/kpè + kì/kí	H	L	H	H	HH	HL	HL	LH	
34	PFTV PERF IND	NF	/	L	ì	í	ká/kpè + kì/kí			H	H	HH	LH	LH	LH	

Aux Pref row 34: }-kà (kpè) -rà/ràbí

Pattern No.	Aspect/Mood	Tense Focus	Aux Pref	1 & 2 sg SP Tone	Subject Prefix 3s	Subject Prefix cpl	Prefix Marker	REDUP SYL. Tone HTV	REDUP SYL. Tone LTV	Stem Tone HTV 1	Stem Tone HTV 2	Stem Tone HTV 3	Stem Tone LTV 1	Stem Tone LTV 2	Stem Tone LTV 3	Suff
35	PFTV PERF IND	NF	v	]-kà (kpɛ́) -rà/ràbí	]	í		H	L		HL	HL	HL	HL	HL	HL
36	IMPF PERF IND	NF	/	]-kà (kpɛ́) -rá/rábè	L	]	í	kí			H	H	HH	LH	LH	HL
37	IMPF PERF IND	NF	v	]-kà (kpɛ́) -rà/ràbè	L	]	í	kí	H	L	HL	HL	HL	HL	HL	HL
38	PFTV IND DEL-NEG (sg)	NF	v		L	]	/	kà	HL	HL	HL	HL	HL	HL	HL	HL
39	PFTV IND DEL-NEG (pl)	NF	v		L	]	∅	kpɛ́	H	L	HL	HL	HL	HL	HL	HL

Appendix 179

LTV examples of the verb patterns

The numbers correspond to the Pattern Numbers in the chart. All examples are of the low tone verb *tàp* 'put'.[54]

1. ékàtâpbè/gè[55]   not putting
2. ékàkîbè/gè ítăp   not putting (not to be putting)
3. ékàkîbè/gè ítàtâp   not PUTTING (not to be PUTTING)
4. kàtăp   don't put
5. kàtàtâp   don't PUT
6. kàkîtăp   don't be putting
7. kàkîtàtâp   don't be PUTTING
8. íkàtăp   let him/her not put
9. íkàtàtâp   let him/her not PUT
10. íkàkîtăp   let him/her not be putting
11. íkàkîtàtâp   let him/her not be PUTTING
12. kpòmótàp   if s/he didn't put
13. kpòmótàtâp   if s/he didn't PUT
14. kpòmókítàp   if s/he were not putting
15. kpòmókítàtâp   if s/he were not PUTTING
16. ìkpôtâp   s/he will not put
17. ìkpôtàtâp   s/he will not PUT
18. ìkpó!kítàp   s/he will be putting
19. ìkpó!kítàtâp   s/he will not be PUTTING
20. ìká/kpóbôtàp   s/he is not going to put
21. ìká/kpóbôtàtâp   s/he is not going to PUT
22. ìká/kpóbôkîtàp   s/he is not going to be putting
23. ìká/kpóbôkîtàtâp   s/he is not going to be PUTTING
24. ìká/kpóbônĭtàp   s/he does not intend to put
25. ìká/kpóbônĭtàtâp   s/he does not intend to PUT
26. ìká/kpóbônĭkítàp   s/he does not intend to be putting
27. ìká/kpóbônĭkítàtâp   s/he does not intend to be PUTTING
28. kpôtâpbé   the place (or time) s/he would not put (one who would not put)
29. íkàtâpbè/gè   place/when s/he did not put (one who did not put)
30. ìkâtăp   s/he did not put
31. ìkâtàtâp   s/he did not PUT and ...

---

[54]As in an HTV examples, the reader is advised to refer to the chart as he reads the examples. There is no space here to label the examples for aspect, perfect, tense, mood, and focus; these are already done in the chart. High tone verb examples are not given, eg.; the verb *sí* 'go'. Their tone patterns are given in the chart for a guide.

[55]Patterns 1–3 are participial forms used in place of infinitives.

32.	ìkákìtăp	s/he does not habitually put
33.	ìkákìtàtâp	s/he does not habitually PUT
34.	ìkàrâbè ìtăp	(whether) s/he has not put
35.	ìkàrâbè ìtàtâp	(whether) s/he has not PUT
36.	ìkàrâbè ìkítăp	(whether) s/he has not been putting
37.	ìkàrâbè ìkìtátâp	(whether) s/he has not been PUTTING
38.	ìkàtâtâp	s/he has not yet put (it)
39.	kpètâtâp	they have not yet put (it)

References

Aaron, Bassey U. 1979. The study of the different religious denominations in Okoroete clan (Eastern Andoni) in Ikot Abasi Local Government Area of the Cross River State of Nigeria. An unpublished Term Paper submitted to the Department of Religious Studies, College of Education, Uyo, in partial fulfillment of the requirements for the award of the National Certificate in Education.

Aaron, Uche E. 1983. Interpropositional relations in Obolo. M.A. thesis, University of Texas at Arlington.

──── . 1996/97. The category of number Obolo in verbal morphology. Journal of West African Languages, (26)(1):49–76.

────. (forthcoming). Obolo (Andoni) orthography. To appear in E. N. Emenajọ (ed.), Orthographies of Nigerian Languages, Manual 6. Federal Ministry of Education, Lagos.

Anderson, Lloyd. 1982. The 'perfect' as a universal and as a language-particular category. In Paul J. Hopper and Sandra A. Thompson (eds.), 227–64.

Anderson, Stephen C. 1979. Verb structure of Aghem. In Larry M. Hyman (ed.), Aghem grammatical structure: With special reference to noun classes, tense-aspect and focus marking. Southern California occasional papers in linguistics 7, 73–136. Los Angeles: University of Southern California.

────. 1980. Tense/aspect in Ngyemboon-Bamileke. Cotonou: Summer Institute of Linguistics.

────── and Bernard Comrie, eds. 1992. Tense and aspect in eight languages of Cameroon. Summer Institute of Linguistics and the University of Texas at Arlington Publications in Linguistics 99. Dallas.

Beekman, John, John Callow, and Michael Kopesec. 1981. The semantic structure analysis of written communication. Dallas: Summer Institute of Linguistics.

Bendor-Samuel, John. 1989. Niger-Congo languages: A classification and description of Africa's largest language family. New York: University Press of America.

Binnick, Robert I. 1991. Time and the verb: A guide to tense and aspect. New York: Oxford University Press.

Burquest, Donald A. 1992. An introduction to the use of aspect in Hausa narrative. In Shin Ja J. Hwang and William Merrifield (eds), Language in context: Essays for Robert E. Longacre, 393–418. Summer Institute of Linguistics and theUniverstiy of Texas at Arlington Publications in Linguistics 107. Dallas.

Bybee, Joan L. 1985. Morphology: A study of the relation between meaning and form. Amsterdam: John Benjamins.

────── and Öesten Dahl. 1989. The creation of tense and aspect systems in the languages of the world. Studies in Language 13(1):51–103.

──────, Revere Perkins, and William Pagliuca. 1994. The evolution of grammar: Tense, aspect, and modality in the languages of the world. Chicago: University of Chicago Press.

Callow, Kathleen and John C. Callow. 1992. Text as a purposeful communication: A meaning-based analysis. In Mann and Thompson (eds.), Discourse description: Diverse linguistic analysis of a fund-raising letter, 5–38. Amsterdam: John Benjamins.

Chung, Sandra and Alan Timberlake. 1985. Tense, aspect and mood. In Timothy Shopen (ed.), Language typology and syntactic description, vol. 3, 202–258. Cambridge: Cambridge University Press.

Chvany, Catherine V. 1985. Backgrounded perfectives and plot line imperfectives (Towards a theory of grounding in text). In Flier and Tiblerlake (eds.), 247–73.

──────. 1990. Verbal aspect, discourse saliency, and the so-called "perfect of result" in modern Russian. In Nils B. Thelin (ed.), 213–35.

Comrie, Bernard. 1976. Aspect: An introduction to the study of verbal aspect and related problems. Cambridge University Press.

──────. 1985. Tense. Cambridge University Press.

Croft, William. 1990. Typology and universals. Cambridge University Press.

Dahl, Östen. 1985. Tense and aspect systems. Oxford: Basil Blackwell.

Dahlgren, Kathleen. 1988. Naive semantics for natural language understanding. Boston: Kluwer Academic Publishers.

Dry, H. 1981. Sentence aspect and the movement of narrative time. Text 1:233–40.

———. 1983. The movement of narrative time. Journal of Literary Semantics 12(2):19–53.

———. 1992. Foregrounding: An assessment. In Shin Ja J. Hwang and William R. Merrifield (eds.), Language in context: Essays for Robert E. Longacre, 393–418. Summer Institute of Linguistics and the University of Texas at Arlingtion Publications in Linguistics 107. Dallas

Ehrlich, Susan. 1987. Aspect, foregrounding and point of view. In van Dijk, Text 7(4):363–76.

Enene, Enene N. 1998. Comparative inflectional morphology of the Obolo dialects. Masters Thesis. Port Harcourt: Universtiy of Port Harcourt.

Ejituwu, Nkparom C. 1991. A history of Obolo (Andoni) in the Niger delta. Oron: Manson Publishing.

Faraclas, Nicholas G. 1984a. A grammar of Obolo. Bloomington: Indiana University Linguistics Club.

———. 1984b. Tone, stress, and the Obolo focus system. Journal of African Languages and Linguistics 6:127–46.

Fleischman, Suzanne. 1985. Discourse functions of tense-aspect oppositions in narrative: Toward a theory of grounding. Linguistics 23:851–82.

———. 1990. Tense and narrativity: From medieval performance to modern French. Austin: University of Texas Press.

———. 1991. Toward a theory of tense-aspect in narrative discourse. Santa Barbara: University of California Colloquium.

Flier, Michael S. and Alan Timberlake, eds. 1985. The scope of Slavic aspect. University of California, Los Angeles Slavic Studies 12. Columbus: Slavica.

Forsyth, James. 1970. A grammar of aspect: Usage and meaning in the Russian verb. Studies in modern languages. Cambridge University Press.

Fries, Peter. 1983. On the status of theme in English: Arguments from discourse. In Janos S. Petïfi and Emel Sözer (eds.), Micro and macro connexity of texts. Hamburg: Helmut Buske Verlag.

Givón, T. 1987. Beyond foreground and background. In Russell Tomlin (ed.), Coherence and grounding in discourse. Typological Studies in Language 11, 177–88. Amsterdam: John Benjamins.

———. 1990. Syntax: A functional-typological introduction Vol. II. Amsterdam: John Benjamins.

Greenberg, Joseph H. 1974. Language typology: A history and analytic overview. Janus Liguarum, Series Minor, 59. The Hague: Mouton.

Grimes, Joseph E. 1975. The thread of discourse. The Hague: Mouton.

Halliday, Michael A. K., and Ruqaiya Hasan. 1976. Cohesion in English. London: Longmans.

Herring, Susan. 1991. Functions of the verb in Tamil narration. Ph.D. dissertation. Berkeley: University of California.

Hopper, Paul J. 1979a. Some observations on the typology of focus and aspect in narrative language. Studies in Language 3(1):37–64.

———. 1979b. Aspect and foregrounding in discourse. In Talmy Givón (ed.), Discourse and Syntax. Syntax and Semantics 12, 213–42. New York: Academic Press.

——— (ed). 1982a. Tense-aspect: Between semantics and pragmatics. Typological studies in language 1. Amsterdam: John Benjamins.

———. 1982b. Aspect between discourse and grammar: An introductory essay for the volume. In Paul J. Hopper and Sandra A. Thompson (eds.), 3–18.

——— and Sandra A. Thompson. 1980. Transitivity in grammar and discourse. Language 56:251–99.

——— and ———, (eds.) 1982. Studies in transitivity. Syntax and Semantics 15, 241–59. New York: Academic Press.

Johnson, Marion. 1981. A unified theory of tense and aspect. In Philip J. Tedeschi and Annie Zaenen (eds), Tense and aspect. Syntax and Semantics 14, 145–75.

Jones, Larry B. and Linda K. Jones. 1984. Verb morphology in discourse structure in Mesoamerican languages. In Longacre (ed.), Theory and application in processing texts in non-Indoeuropean languages, 25–48. Hamburg: Helmut Buske.

Kamp, Hans. 1985. Context, thought and communication. Proceedings of the Aristotelian Society 85:239–61.

Labov, William. 1972. Language in the inner city. Philadelphia: University of Pennsylvania Press.

——— and J. Waletzky. 1967. Narrative analysis: Oral versions of personal experience. In June Helm (ed.), Essays on the verbal and visual arts, 12–44. Seattle: University of Washington Press.

Lee, Hyo Sang. 1991. Tense, aspect, and modality: A discourse-pragmatic analysis of verbal affixes in Korean from a typological perspective. Ph.D. dissertation. Los Angeles: University of Los Angeles.

Lehmann, Winfred P. 1973. A structural principle of language and its implications. Language 49:47–66.

Lewis, David. 1972. General semantics. In D. Davidson and G. Harmon (eds.), Semantics of natural language. Dordrecht: Reidel.

Li, Charles N., Sandra A. Thompson, and R. McMillan Thompson. 1982. The discourse motivation for the perfect aspect: The Mandarin particle LE. In Paul J. Hopper and Sandra A. Thompson (eds.), 19–42.

Longacre, Robert E. 1968. Philippine languages: Discourse, paragraph and sentence structure. Santa Ana: Summer Institute of Linguistics.
———. 1972. Hierarchy and universality of discourse constituents in New Guinea Languages. Washington, D.C.: Georgetown University Press.
———. 1982. Verb ranking and the constituency structure of discourse. Journal of the Linguistic Association of the Southwest 5:77-202.
———. 1983. The grammar of discourse. New York: Plenum.
———. 1989. Two hypotheses regarding text generation and analysis. Discourse Processes 12:413-60.
Lyons, John. 1968. Introduction to theoretical linguistics, Cambridge University Press.
———. 1977. Semantics. Cambridge University Press.
Mann, William C. and Sandra A. Thompson, (eds.) 1987. Rhetorical structure theory: A theory of text organization. Marina del Rey: University of Southern California, Information Sciences Institute.
McArthur, Harry S. 1979. The role of aspect in distinguishing Aguacatec discourse types. In Linda K. Jones (ed.), Discourse studies in Mesoamerican languages 1, 97-121. Dallas: Summer Institute of Linguistics and University of Texas at Arlington Publications in Linguistics 58. Dallas.
McCoard, Robert. 1978. The English perfect: Tense choice and pragmatic inferences. Amsterdam: North Holland.
Rafferty, Ellen. 1979. Aspect in conversational Indonesian. In Paul J. Hopper and Sandra A. Thompson, 65-87.
Reichman, Rachel. 1985. Getting computers to talk like you and me. Cambridge, Mass.: MIT Press.
Reichenbach, Hans. 1947. Elements of symbolic logic. New York: MacMillan.
Sapir, Edward. 1921. Language, an introduction to the study of speech. New York: Harcourt, Bruce, and World.
Schram, Terry L. 1979. Tense, tense embedding, and theme in discourse in Mazatec of Jalapa de Díaz. In Linda K. Jones (ed.), Discourse studies in Mesoamerican languages 1,141-67. Dallas: Summer Institute of Linguistics and University of Texas at Arlington Publications in Linguistics 58. Dallas.
Smith, Carlota S. 1983. A theory of aspectual choice. Language 59(3):479-501.
———. 1991. The parameter of aspect. Dordrecht: Kluwer Academic Publishers.
Thelin, Nils B. 1990a. Verbal aspect in discourse: On the state of the art. In Nils B. Thelin (ed.), 3-88.

———. 1990b. On the concept of time: Prolegomena to a theory of aspect and tense in narrative discourse. In Nils B. Thelin (ed.), 91–129.

——— (ed.). 1990c. Verbal aspect in discourse: Contributions to the semantic of time and temporal perspective in Slavic and non-Slavic languages. Amsterdam: John Benjamins.

Thompson, Sandra A. 1987. "Subordination" and narrative event structure. In Russell Tomlin (ed.), Coherence and grounding in discourse. Typological Studies in Languages 11, 435–54. Amsterdam: John Benjamins.

van Peer, Willie. 1986. Stylistics and psychology: Investigations of foregrounding. London: Croom Helm.

Vendler, Zeno. 1967. Verbs and times. In Linguistics and Philosophy, 97–121. Ithaca: Cornell University Press.

Wallace, Stephen. 1982. Figure and ground: The interrelationships of linguistic categories. In Paul J. Hopper and Sandra A. Thompson (ed.), 201–23.

Watters, John R. 1979. Focus in Aghem: A study of its formal correlates and typology. In Larry M. Hyman (ed.), Aghem grammatical structure: With special reference to noun classes, tense-aspect and focus marking. Southern California Occasional Papers in Linguistics 7, 137–95. Los Angeles: University of Southern California.

Waugh, Linda R. 1990. Discourse functions of tense-aspect in French: Dynamic synchrony. In Nils B. Thelin (ed.), 159–87.

Woisetschlaeger, Eric F. 1985. A semantic theory of the English auxiliary system. New York: Garland.

www.ingramcontent.com/pod-product-compliance
Lightning Source LLC
Chambersburg PA
CBHW070330230426
43663CB00011B/2269